Head over Heels

First published in Great Britain in 2010 by Moonrise Press, Ludlow.

© Christopher Martin 2010

ISBN 978-0-9539561-5-9

Printed in Great Britain by Cromwell Press Group.

Head Over Heels

In the hot seat at Millfield School

CHRISTOPHER MARTIN

MOONRISE PRESS

For Denny Brock, who taught me how to teach

Si jeunesse savait, si vieillesse pouvait.

Preface

One of the privileges of my time in politics is that I have been able to learn from people I might never otherwise have met, and what those people have said has been influential on my own thinking. Christopher Martin is one such person.

Christopher's teaching experiences are a world away from my own. Yet getting to know him, you very quickly learn that the passion for learning, the joy of seeing young people succeed, and the daily challenges facing any institution that brings together hundreds of young people and adults, have remarkable similarities no matter where the school.

Christopher Martin's account of his time as Head of one of the country's leading public schools is in part a story of a talented and committed teacher and school leader, who has given a working lifetime and more to guiding young people as they move from childhood to adulthood. The joy he expresses when a young person succeeds, the care he takes with a parent who is concerned, his belief in an education system that can respond to the strengths and needs of each child, coupled with a clear understanding of the consequences of failure, mark Christopher Martin out as a gifted educator.

Yet this book is more than a record of one person's time as a teacher. It is a first hand account of leadership in one of the country's best known and most successful schools. Millfield was founded by a 'far-sighted entrepreneur' from India who bequeathed it strong international and tolerant values and a commitment to the broadest definition of education.

The school now has a national and an international reputation. Christopher's book is not, however, an easy rehearsal of its achievements but an honest account of the challenges and joys of leading a multi-racial, multi-faith boarding school.

This account gives you everything: the successes and disappointments, the joys and the tragedies, the frustrations and let downs, as well as the battles fought and won. Most of all, it is Christopher Martin's own personal story that he shares with us and from which we can learn as well as enjoy. It is open and comprehensive and he tells it just as he experienced it.

You cannot know Christopher Martin without appreciating the role that young people and Millfield School have played in his life and he in theirs. This book is not just a valuable insight into life in an educational hot seat, but testament to the power of teachers to change lives.

Estelle Morris
Former Secretary of State for Education

Foreword

I fell into teaching quite by accident. After National Service with the 10th Gurkhas in Malaya, and having achieved a modest degree from St Andrews in modern languages, I found myself facing the long summer of 1963 with no clear view of how to make a living that autumn. Fortunately, a friend drew my attention to an unexpected vacancy which had just occurred at Westminster School. Since it was so late in the day, I was the only candidate, which helps to explain why I was offered the post, for at that time I had no teaching qualification. The salary was £900 p.a., payable termly in arrears.

Westminster could scarcely have been a more propitious place at which to land. Bright, inquisitive, challenging boys, highly motivated colleagues and London on the doorstep. I stayed for thirteen years, eight of them as a housemaster, interrupted only by an exchange year at Philips Exeter Academy in New Hampshire, which gave me many new perspectives on the elusive art of good teaching.

In 1979 I was appointed Headmaster of Bristol Cathedral School, a small ex-Direct Grant grammar school. Just as I had had no qualifications when arriving at Westminster, here too I arrived with no training for such a post. I just had to get on with the job by trial and, often initially, by error. However, the school had an inner institutional strength, which enabled it to survive my early ministrations. We added essential new buildings on the tiny footprint we owned and built also on our sound academic and good musical reputations. With colleagues who knew what they were about, I found time to become involved outside the school as chairman of the Choir Schools' Association and of a working party, representing all the UK's secondary heads, on increasing teacher numbers in maths and physics. I also took a six-week sabbatical in East Africa on behalf of Students Partnership Worldwide, founding as a result the Textbooks for Africa Project, which delivered over a million unwanted O-Level books to schools in thirteen African countries.

Coming from a small, urban, boys, 11–18, selective day school with a religious foundation, it was a huge risk for Millfield's governors to appoint me as headmaster to the biggest co-educational, rural, 13–18, non-selective, multi-faith boarding school in the UK. I moved there in 1990, as the school's first outside appointment to this role.

Millfield had been established in 1935 by Jack 'Boss' Meyer who had brought the sons of five maharajas over with him and his wife Joyce from India. He was an astonishingly far-sighted educational entrepreneur. His idiosyncratic, flamboyant style would have had today's health and safety executives reaching for the smelling salts. With promethean energy and a cheerfully reckless approach to prevailing pedagogic theories, he established an ethos founded on the assumption that every young person had special gifts and that it was therefore the school's job to lay on courses and facilities which would allow these gifts to flourish. Today's heavily controlled curriculum would have been anathema to him. His pupils, without exception as far as I know, were and remain utterly devoted to him. Sadly he died in my first year, but I met him twice and will always remember the way in which he would recall four or five salient facts about every person who went through his school. He was succeeded by his deputy Colin Atkinson, who during his twenty-year tenancy provided the school with a sound infrastructure more recognizable to modern eyes than Boss's unpredictable approach.

To me, the sheer scale of things at Millfield was at first bewildering. There were 1,250 pupils, 15% of whom came from fifty different countries, 28 boarding houses, 190 full time tutors teaching forty-eight different A-Level courses, 40 competitive sports, and over 100 out-of-school activities. But while those numbers are big, classes and tutor groups were amazingly small— seldom more than twelve in a class. There were, for example, over twenty sets in the first three years in all main subjects. I once taught the twenty-first French set in Year 9 and probably learnt more about teaching them than they learnt French from me.

All tutors had a small group of pupils for whose academic progress they were responsible, while their houseparents shouldered the pastoral responsibility. All boarding houses had live-in houseparents. While most of these houses were on campus, a sizeable minority were at the end of a bus journey. A fleet of coaches ferried these pupils in to school in the morning for breakfast and home again in the evening for homework, recreation and to sleep. Some of these off-campus houses were lavishly equipped. One had a golf course, a polo pitch and its own church. All tutors were members of at least one academic department and heads of department met me every week to ensure a two-way flow of communication. The executive group comprised the bursar, the deputy head, the head of the prep school and me. The prep school was a couple of miles away at Edgarley Hall and had over 600 pupils, while the pre-prep school in Glastonbury catered for some 100 smaller people. Thus the entire Millfield diaspora was responsible for almost 2,000 pupils at any one time. And thus also rather more than 4,000 parents!

My reasons for believing I had the best job in the world stem from my first morning there. I took my place in the queue for lunch, collected my tray and wandered into the dining hall, looking for somewhere to sit. A group of what turned out to be Fourth Formers budged up to make room, so I joined them. The boy next to me turned, beaming with unfeigned pleasure, and asked, 'How are you enjoying the job, Sir?' I quickly found that this refreshing willingness to treat the headmaster as if he were a fully paid-up member of the human race was widely shared among the majority of pupils, and I'd like to think among tutors as well, though naturally the relationships with them were more complicated.

I lived and breathed Millfield for eight years, but it was only in the last four years that I started to make notes in the evening of the episodes which had made each day memorable in some way to me. Many of these anecdotes are entirely inconsequential, and do not presume to be anything else. I hope they may cumulatively offer some insight, however, into the range of activity facing the head of any big boarding school perhaps, but particularly of this one. I have heard it said that the Head makes a school. This is not true. While he is responsible and thus involved, it is the tutors in their many interactions with pupils every day who really define the success of a school. I would like to acknowledge here the exemplary work of all my colleagues who made Millfield the happy, purposeful place it is. I feel the following pages confirm their success.

Christopher Martin
March 2010

Chapter 1

Sophie's fees are put on a horse

AUGUST 1994. Two weeks to go until the start of the new academic year and already the bizarre events I will always associate with Millfield start to occur even before I've re-established contact with the bottom of my summer holiday in-tray.

There's a big fuss about Ruth, a talented and startlingly beautiful girl from Malaysia with whom Tom, another sixth-former, fell in love last term. It appears that rather than pay for his phone calls from his House here to hers, a distance of a mile or so, he somehow routed them via New York, using his father's American Express Gold card. This did nicely for him, until of course the bill arrived showing a cost of £4,000 for the two-week period in question. Tom's father is incandescent, which seems reasonable. Ruth's father threatens to withdraw her, feeling not unreasonably that, being a strict Muslim, she is too heavily involved with this Headstrong young Brit. I call him to plead her case, offering a move to a billet with an experienced tutor, which will satisfy his anxieties, at least for the moment.

The Village of Education is in full swing, with about 1,000 holiday makers taking part in some 300 courses all over the campus. It is a surprise to encounter a friend, a distinguished Malaysian lawyer, nursing a back injury sustained during his chosen course which is

Circus Skills, having spent the week bending down to retrieve his dropped juggling balls. His trade takes him all over the Pacific Rim and this self-inflicted wound will not help his cause.

Following a spate of thefts from our houses over the summer, the police decide to mount a 24-hour surveillance operation from Holmcroft House on the private house opposite, where our stolen goods and others are thought to be held. This takes some delicate handling as people can only be told of this on a need-to-know basis. What should we tell the cleaners, for instance? That our visitors are just rather inactive lodgers, perhaps, with a penchant for voyeurism?

The Old Millfieldian dinner this year is for those who were here between 1966 and 1980, and to our surprise and delight 120 people show up. The doyen is Nathan Penney (1945 alumnus) from Canada. A bonhomous occasion, of course, with delirium at the new buildings, tinged with regret at the passing of the last of the Nissen huts which had housed them during their school days. Changes at their school are often hard for alumni to accept, though since Millfield is practically synonymous with change, regrets of that kind are rare here. The trick is to nourish affection for the past while cultivating optimism for the future. As an American general said recently, 'If you don't like change you're gonna like irrelevance a helluva lot less.' I am reminded of a fine old boy visiting the Geology Department at Bristol Cathedral School and concluding, 'The world was too young to have fossils when I was at school.'

Fregenet comes to see me. Having left last term, she is now in a quandary, for her father in Geneva has instructed her to return, disregarding her views and conveying his own views, not in person, but over the phone. She is desperate, and I sympathize with her predicament. I manage to get through to her father and have a rather rewarding talk to him in French, during which he was big-hearted enough to see the point about the importance of Fregenet's own views being taken into account. Eventually he promises to make other arrangements. She rewards me with a huge smile.

As she leaves, we are treated to the surreal spectacle of a mobile crane lumbering over the golf course with 'Sheep Piece' clamped firmly in its jaws, heading for its final resting place near the pavilion. This was the GCSE class's project: to reconstruct Henry Moore's massive sculpture to scale before it left Clark's in Street for the USA. It weighs three and a half tons, and stands about twelve feet high, a tribute to ingenuity, tenacity and a lively spirit of adventure in our art department. Pupils have certainly never undertaken anything on this scale before and the result is spectacular. I'm sure it will escape the censure of my senior colleague, Roger Adams, who, at the arrival on site of last year's sculpture project 'Portals', suggested, tongue somewhere in cheek, that it was reminiscent of ironwork rejected by the Gdansk shipyards.

Hassle on the phone with the immigration people at Gatwick, who will not allow our third Virginian Fellow into the country. It's never gone wrong before but there is the poor chap, under lock and key for three hours, on the strength of a newly invented snag. Once we'd secured his release, I cycled over to the preparatory school at Edgarley to see the new girls' boarding house at Berewall Farm, just acquired. This must be the only boarding house in a prep school in the country to boast en-suite bathrooms for all the inmates. That old crack about boarding schools preparing you beautifully for life in prison must be wearing thin now.

The last Friday before the troops return. I took my mother for a quick tour of the current building sites on campus: the theatre, the new swimming pool, the staff room extension, the two additional multi purpose science labs, the Fine Arts centre roof—a second stab at this—and the Village of Education offices. Encouraging stuff, of course, but with the written-in disadvantage that the whole school risks being mistaken for a major industrial development. I also managed a couple of hours with Pepys' Diary, probably the last decent reading time before Christmas.

[3]

Konstantinos and his mother come from Athens, both tall and immensely distinguished. She is a Member of Parliament, as was her husband, who was assassinated some five years ago. I later learnt that Konstantinos first heard of this on television. She is a superb woman who now wants her son to make his own life in our sixth-form. He strikes me as a natural for us, keen to board and to set out on his own journey. His mother clearly respects this in him, knowing nevertheless how much she will miss him at home.

I spend an hour touring Houses with Paul Oddie, the Bursar, trying to find room for ten extra beds and trespassing on the patience and good will of the houseparents involved, who take it in good heart nonetheless. This is followed by another hour with the school solicitor discussing an outrageous fees-in-lieu-of-notice case which looks as though this time it really might get to court. I have no difficulty in sympathising with parents who register complaints while their children are still at school. That's their right, and even their duty if they feel a complaint is warranted. But those who manufacture them after their child has left to avoid fulfilling their contractual obligation to pay a term's fees when they withdraw without warning or consultation—that really tests one's sympathy.

Supper with the new staff at Edgarley, our preparatory school. How young they look! But then so do ours the next day when I welcome them for their induction day. There are nineteen of them; a new chaplain, Heads of Maths and History, both women, and eleven people under the age of twenty five. This shifts the average age of the Common Room a bit and their total age has now subsided since last term by over 400 years. Our newcomers seem full of beans and apprehension in equal measure, which is pretty much how I feel too, as always at the start of a new term. I promise them that it never gets less exciting but perhaps they saw that as a warning. In the evening, watching some of them finding their feet among the 250 teachers and spouses who came to the staff dinner, I sensed how lucky they were. The buzz was happening again, the feeling of barely controlled exhilaration was upon us all. Or upon most of us anyway. A newcomer could not help but feel he'd landed the right way up.

Sunday afternoon; the meeting for all the Lower Sixth and their parents. Anticipation bordering on hysteria or panic, depending on whether you're new or a veteran. All the Heads of Departments are on parade, trying to sort out changes of mind on proposed A-Level courses, crises of confidence, or occasionally exaggerated faith in modest abilities, generated by flattering GCSE results. They look so vulnerable and my heart goes out to them. I remember particularly Marie Braconnier from Paris with her two wide-eyed sisters, also Saleh from Saudi, and Bronson from South Africa on a scholarship who would get to know almost everyone in the school faster than I'd have believed possible, and the great Mat Rochford who told me he wanted to be a teacher at Millfield in due course, and never leave.

The first day of term. I'm practically redundant, apart from launching the 290 people in the Lower Sixth on their introduction to the sixth-form. Having done so, I stayed on to watch my colleague prove to them brilliantly and memorably that two A-Level years reduce in fact to just fifteen days of concentrated work. Jaws dropped. There's nothing like a solid dose of realism with which to get the new school year under way. Back to my study to get a real earful from M. Braconnier, all three of whose stunning daughters started yesterday.

'Je suis scandalisé, M. Martin. Acacia est très décevante. Je suis très déçu...extrêmement anxieux'.

Apparently he thought, for some reason, that all our boarders were housed in private homes. In Street! It's a relief to learn that his girls all seem very happy with the arrangements and have already made plenty of friends.

A delightful Saudi family visited 'just to pay our respects' while leaving their son with us. Mother and sister were both heavily veiled. What an exotic garment a veil can be. They were followed by a Kenyan family who were very keen for a place, but we are 1,292 on roll, 30 more than ever before, and really need withdrawals rather than further entries. Set off for the dining hall at 1.30 and got there at 2.15, such was the bumping into colleagues and pupils.

I had a long phone call with Urska Kakochar's mother in Slovenia, during which I tried to reassure her that after only two nights with us it's too early to capitulate and withdraw her daughter for homesickness. This was followed by a request from the Catholic World Games Committee to come to Millfield in two years' time with 1,200 athletes from all over the world. This on top of last month's request that the World Flying Disc Championships (we are not allowed to call them Frisbees) be held here next year. Watched the riding, including a new star from the USA on her hot horse, and some eighty rugby Foals all galloping about in the sunshine and looking a lot more frisky than some of the horses.

Two long phone calls with Karachi. Babar Lakhani, one of the most affable and laziest of boys I've encountered, is hell-bent on going home to pursue an easier life, and since he's aged 18, we do not find it easy to compel him to stay. Father would have none of this and practically asked me to manacle Babar to his desk. His parents refuse to readmit him to their home. Impasse.

Robert has been here a week and, according to his mother, rang home eventually to let her know how he was. 'I know I'm going to be really homesick, Mum, but I haven't had time to be yet.'

Into breakfast. One of the elite swimmers puts away half a dozen eggs after his hour in the pool without batting an eyelid. Meeting with our new University of Virginia Fellow who wants to leave at Christmas to pursue courses to which he has not previously referred. I take a dim view, but in view of his craven attitude, perhaps it's all for the best. Houseparents and the Senior Matron come to discuss urine testing procedures. The Executive Group then meets me at home over the future of the Village of Education in the light of the Catholic Games and the World Frisbee Championships, now both confirmed. Back to school to sign letters to Lord Grade (will he open our new theatre?), Ben Tan (will he host a recruitment visit to Shanghai?), and to Tim Fok (is there a future for his proposed 'satellite' Millfield in his new city, Nansha, in China?). Home again late to write a talk for the Headmasters' Conference annual meeting on HIV/AIDS, and to compose guidelines for houseparents on targeted urine testing for drugs.

After a two hour meeting with the architects on the theatre we went into the auditorium, my first chance to feel the shape of things inside. It's going to be superb; there's a real sense of intimacy there which will, I hope, tend to make even the most reluctant pupil feel included. Then another attritional Appeal meeting. We're only half way to our target of £1.5 million. I got tetchy when the consultant raised the stakes again. I did not chair it well and everything got pretty turgid. A relief to leave to visit Holmcroft for a couple of hours with my wife Julia. Bayard Barron, the Head of House, took us round so that we visited all fifty boys in their natural habitat without disturbing their prep too badly, I hope. Their welcome is heartening indeed. Even if this is the most exhausting thing we do on a weekly basis, and it is, the reward of finding young people prepared to chat and joke in a relaxed way on their home patch while never overstepping the invisible line into overfamiliarity is hugely rewarding. With twenty-eight boarding houses to visit, it's a bit like the Forth Bridge and it takes us almost a year to visit them all, but it's entirely worthwhile.

Free fall all day. Discussion on the Green Council, to my General Studies lesson, to the Executive Group on building priorities for 1996, to the Heads of Departments meeting, to Joe Peake, the Director of Studies, to discuss GNVQ courses for next year over a sandwich, to the Prefects Meeting with all eighty of them, to two seniors, Ceri and Tamara, to talk to me of their anxieties—well founded—on eating disorders, to an anguished father removing his very pleasant but lonely son, partly because of his mother who suffers mental illness—a harrowing interview, to Sally and Gorab hot foot from Nepal to discuss our proposed Millfield project in Pokhara, to the school counsellor with several thorny problems, mostly concerning new pupils who are finding it difficult to settle in. And at 6.00 to the in-tray.

On return from the HMC annual conference, there is the spectre of an expulsion for cannabis, which quickly undoes all the good that contact with friends for three days at HMC had achieved. This is not all, however. There is also the unprecedented threat from a parent of a swimmer to sue us for our 'incorrect' training methods. It turns out that he's already successfully done something similar at Norwich and presumably thinks he's on some sort of gravy train.

A Nigerian father with the unlikely name of Doherty comes to see me to seek a guarantee that his son will get a university place in five years' time, despite assurances to the contrary from Edgarley. Some tough talking along the lines of 'read my lips' ensues. This is followed immediately by an extraordinary family, where the father is seventy-seven and the mother forty, who want to withdraw their daughter. She had been homesick in the early days of term but is so no longer. They were all so appreciative of the school that I simply could not fathom why the move could be contemplated at all. I urged a stay of execution and won it. We'll see. Before I could catch my breath from this, Jenny, my secretary, ushered in an admirable father who did not expect to be alive in a month and who naturally wanted to sort out his son's education before he died. It is the most poignant moment of the week by far. I have the feeling afterwards that a hundred years of in-service training could not prepare one for such a morning.

Dreadful news from Claire Shimell, our counsellor, of the two Lower Sixth girls who have been to see her about a rape they each endured during the holiday, both it seems at the hands of friends of their families. The circumstances, and of course the names, are not for me to know, but the fact that two young people in our midst should have suffered like this is deeply disturbing. It is reassuring that they are in touch with someone who knows how to help them, and it serves to increase one's respect for our seniors as a group, but there is a terrible sense of impotence in not being able to help those who, for good reasons, want their anonymity respected.

Three pupils in quick succession this morning, including one who wants me to agree to his returning to Saudi against his parents' instructions; answer: no. Then a posse of sixth-formers who want to set up another Young Enterprise group with four different projects; answer, yes; and finally the irresistible Zoe with a new charity request for a non-uniform day; answer, yes, as always. A grilling follows from two sets of efficient and well-briefed parents with children in tow, and then straight into the School Council, all sixty of them, who have prepared a long list of ingenious questions which they put with incomparable tact. David Rosser, who chairs the meeting with unflappable good humour, manages to concede half their points, while ensuring that no real ground is given where it could never be reclaimed.

The *Today* programme reports the attempted assassination in Mexico of the father of Diego Ortega, who is in Etonhurst House. His friend next to him was killed. Teachers are alerted to ensure that Diego is able to cope with this during the course of the day. Interviewed by three girls for their radio project. Unfortunately, half an hour passes before they realize the batteries in their tape recorder are flat, so we schedule another meeting. Meet Richard Ellison, John Major's favourite England cricketer, who is a possible candidate for our new post as Master i/c Cricket. Into the Salle to debate the motion 'Drug tests are a step towards a police state', which Anna Saunders and I, to our surprise, win in front of an animated audience of about one hundred. In retrospect I cannot remember which side we were on. That's embarrassing.

A good moment today when I took a visiting speaker on Europe into lunch. Having armed ourselves with our trays, we sat down by good fortune next to Chris from Germany, Costas from Greece, Marie from France and several home-grown sixth-formers—as good a bunch of young Europeans as I can imagine. Our speaker claimed to have found a new faith in the European ideal in their company over the bread and butter pudding.

This appears to have been a ninety-seven hour week, probably because of leading the HMC inspection team at Clifton College, leaving all of us visitors with a mixed feeling of achievement and exhaustion, though no doubt only the latter is felt at Clifton. It was their first inspection ever I believe, and some of the staff were clearly unused to having visitors, especially fellow professionals, in their classes. There was a mixture of resentment and adrenalin which occasionally manifested itself in over activity. One linguist was so hyper that he bounded about his class firing questions at the boys and then, to their bewilderment, answering them himself. My team comprised a dozen experienced teachers from various HMC schools, one of whom revealed detective skills of a high order when, as the inspection week began, he tied thread between certain chairs in the library. He checked them again at the end. The threads were unbroken. This did raise doubts about the school's claim that the library was 'in constant use.'

Back on Friday night just in time for the House song competition in the Jubilee Sports Hall—the best night of the year, with over 700 singers and a level of mutual support rarely experienced on such a scale. Excitement levels run high: winning matters, after all the work that has been put in. Kate Rees is awarded 'Best Conductor', to universal acclaim. Home eventually to find a message that my mother has suffered a stroke, that she's in hospital and will miss her eightieth birthday celebrations tomorrow. When we see her in London early the next day, her first words are, 'I've been misbehaving'—the best words I could have hoped for in the circumstances.

Today, two pieces of bad news even before the day has properly begun. The first is that a girl has told our counsellor of abuse she has suffered at home. This must be put to social services and our procedures followed to the letter. At this early stage I am not allowed to know the girl's identity, but this will change if it is decided that there is substance in the story and that the poor girl is in any kind of jeopardy. The second blow is that Alison, our excellent Director of Riding, has been lured away by Sir George Bamford to work privately for him. She gave him a good deal of time when he flew in by helicopter to scope the school for his son. This is how he repays us. I will not stand in Alison's way, even if I could, but I write to complain that effectively bribing people to break their contract is not acceptable in schools even if it is common practice in Sir George's line of business. He replies politely but is unrepentant.

By contrast, the good news is that Richard Ellison will come to run our cricket, that the World Flying Disc Championships have been awarded to us in the teeth of competition from USA, UK and European Universities, that Grange House won the cross-country for the first time ever, that my mother can come to stay on her release from hospital and, intriguingly, that I am reappointed to the Privy Council Education Committee.

Fourteen appointments in the diary today, excluding the routine things, one of which was the final meeting on finishes in the theatre—colour, landscaping, lights, curtains; very exciting to sense how it will all soon look. Also a goodbye to the organizer of the exhibition of Zimbabwean sculpture that has so embellished the grounds since the early summer. These vast and wondrous works have been part of our immediate landscape for so long that we'll feel naked without them.

At the Executive Group meeting on minor and major capital expenditure for the coming year, the Bursar produces two comprehensive lists of possible and of necessary works. We manage to knock £100k off the total at one point but weaken, feeling we have been too brutal, and put £40k back on again to transform the rifle range into an auxiliary dining area.

A quad from a houseparent, Kim Ridgeon, lightens my day. He tells of a parent of a girl in his House who thoughtfully left £50 with him in safekeeping for her daughter's pocket money, but omitted to tell him that she was slipping £650 to her daughter in cash 'for those little hidden extras.'

Don Foster, Liberal Democrat spokesman on Education, came to give the Friday lecture, which he did brilliantly. I was impressed by his communications network, which managed to get a leaked copy of the Prime Minister's speech to the Tory party conference to him over a cup of coffee in my study.

Saturday afternoon, one of the best times of the week, when I can get out and watch the pupils in action. I saw some squash, a judo class, fencing, the Somerset netball championships, hockey against Bath University, and tennis. The mismatch of the afternoon was the game, at their suggestion, between the Jersey under-21 girls and our boys' hockey side, which we won 14-1.

A most manipulative girl has stirred such trouble in her boarding house that she will have to go. Even then, it is only when she has been suspended that other girls start to come forward to express their fear of her. Her room-mate, who we had thought was a good friend, described her as 'evil.' Both her mother and the mother of the excellent head-girl bend my ear, the first for acting against her daughter, the second for not acting soon enough to protect hers. It is an emotionally draining day for me, but has clearly been far worse for far longer for the others involved. Half-term comes in the nick of time, though as we take off with our sailing pals for a week afloat on the Ionian Sea, the news that seven people have been killed by rain in Athens does not strike us as a promising meteorological omen.

A tough return, especially on the first day back from so much outdoor hedonism in Greece, with a world record of nineteen entries in the diary. It was a few years ago that the Chairman of Governors

[12]

Ralph Clark asked me to list all the appointments I had in a week to get the feel of the volume of things coming past my desk. I counted 110 and never dared count them again. The best moment today was when Penny Vincenzi, an elegant, cosmopolitan woman and best selling author visiting as a prospective parent, met in my room another prospective parent, a plasterer from Bristol, and discovered that they had a kibbutz in Israel in common: one had born on the kibbutz and the other had a daughter living there. There are, I guess, few contexts in which the two could have encountered each other, and it seems entirely right that a school should bring them together, where their daughters will share so much in the coming years. Diversity is a key to all good education.

Further meetings with Jonathon Mindu, a visiting teacher from Uganda on an exchange I'd arranged eight years earlier while at Bristol Cathedral School; with a Mr Badr from the UAE, thinking aloud and inconclusively about a possible twinning arrangement there; with the Green Council debating our environmental policies in school; and finally with two pupils back from suspension, who promised predictably not to err or stray again. Neither of them sound particularly convincing but we must give them another try and see how their protestations of future innocence work out in practice. Finally, around seven o'clock, a trip out with Mike Gilfillan and the chaplain to select the electronic organ for the theatre at an unlikely organ shop in a private home near Weston-super-Mare. This turns out to be far enough away from neighbours for Mike to be able to let rip with all the decibels he could elicit from a whole battery of likely machines—an ear-splitting and thoroughly cathartic experience.

Another really unpleasant letter from a father accusing the school of untold horrors particularly involving bullying, a long list of sins of commission and of omission. But he still refuses to come and find out the situation for himself. He has never once been to the school, even before selecting us as the right place for his son, let alone the House, and has never met his son's roommates nor his housemaster. There is no evidence to support any of his claims, least of all from his son who has no complaints about life at school, it seems—only about life at home. It is stomach turning, until one realizes that this is a father who spends much of his time abroad and who may have succumbed to the 'absent father' syndrome—trying to over-compensate for his absence on the rare occasions when he pitches up on the home front.

Abbi Mnatzaganian, a distinguished Arabist and modern linguist, tells me that Helen has written 'the definitive essay on Antigone.' Coming from him, this must be taken seriously, for Abbi's standards are sky high. It's a happy fluke, then, that I find myself sitting next to Helen at lunch and can find out more from her of her interest in Anouilh, which clearly runs deep. She is emerging as something of a star. Later from the sublime to the unhappy. Despite nine phone calls from his father in Kuwait begging for a stay of execution, I have no option but to expel Hamad for various serious offences, which have exhausted the patience of houseparent, form tutor and head of year alike, all of whom have spent hours with him. The only silver lining is that home is where the poor boy really wants to be. I hope he finds a warm reception there at an emotional temperature he can tolerate.

Today a parent takes the trouble to come to see me to tell me that he attributes his son's recent graduation success to the foundations laid down in our classrooms during his career here. It turned out that Marjorie Brunt, his Physics teacher, had fired him with a real passion for learning. 'It's all down to Mrs Brunt,' he said. Yet only fifteen minutes earlier, at a staff development interview, Marjorie had been agonising over whether she ever got any satisfactory results from her teaching. A wonderful coincidence which I draw to her attention as soon as I can.

Almost the worst of all scenarios. Claire, our counsellor, tells me of a fourth-year girl who has had intercourse at home at the weekend. I am, of course, not allowed to know her name at this stage. They took precautions but the condom broke and she may be pregnant. She refuses to tell her parents. No teacher is thought to know but apparently a number of pupils do. The usual tests will be conducted by the medical staff. The boy's identity is not known. It's not even clear if he is a member of the school. Luckily the tests turn out to be negative. Claire will keep in close touch and still hopes to persuade the girl to talk it all through with her parents.

7.30 a.m. Talked to Janet Barker, head of chemistry, about inspection processes.

8.00 Usual meeting with David Rosser.

8.30 Took Upper Sixth assembly.

9.00 Phone calls returned from yesterday.

9.30 With Ron Smith, ex-Avon Music Advisor, helping me with Director of Music appointments.

10.15 Sat in on the music lesson given by the first candidate.

11.00 Saw him in action with the choir.

11.15 Gave out notices in the staff common room.

11.30 With Bev Dovey, head of games.

12.00 p.m. Interviewed first applicant for DoM post.

12.30 And the second.

1.10. Drinks with applicants and the department.

1.30 Lunch with them, plus key music pupils.

2.00 Old Millfieldian from Canada, one of the first pupils to have been admitted here.

2.20. Sat in on another music lesson.

2.45 Discussion with Ron and David on the candidates seen to date. Deadlock!

3.30 With DSS inspectors concerning our procedures in general and our abused girl in particular.

4.15 Meeting with the ten prefect team leaders.

5.15 Saw the parents of Marie-Claire who are in the middle of their divorce.

6.00 The in-tray, for the first time today.

8.00 The fifth-form concert, a very refreshing respite at this stage in such a day.

9.30 Home for phone discussions on the progress this far with the Director of Music post, progress which is not easy to pin down at this admittedly early stage in the game.

A cheering letter from a parent on a Gary Larson card. 'I am in a bit of a panic. I realize I have just put some of Sophie's fees for next term on a horse.' From the tenor of the rest of the letter, it appeared that the horse had not only failed to win, but had had a hard time coming in last, and this would entail some delay in clearing their account, and would I kindly smile nicely at the Bursar for her. Irresistible.

The Governors' Education Committee had a really good discussion on fundamentals in the wake of our predictably lower GCSE results this year. These had been lowered by the introduction two years previously of our science and foreign-language-for-all policy. Given the enormous spread of ability of the children we welcome here, many had found these disciplines demanding. Staff, too, had had to come to terms with new cohorts of youngsters whom they had not expected to teach before. A learning experience for everyone, therefore. The question came down to whether we want to educate children broadly or reduce the number of exams they take to enhance our statistical results. Arguments for the former prevailed, as they should do at Millfield, but we know we will have to be prepared to make more exceptions for those with special learning difficulties for whom the increased timetable can prove too much. Having myself recently taught the 21st French set out of 21 in the Third Form, I know how hard some pupils find a modern language.

A small fire in the common room of Millfield House overnight is reported on local radio as 'half of Millfield School destroyed.' Putting the record straight was followed by the immensely saddening business of having to say goodbye to a poor, bereft sixth-former, new to us this term. He had been compelled to return after the half-term holiday by his father, whose chauffeur had forced him physically into the car, locked the doors, driven him to Street and manhandled him into his House. The boy has been traumatized by this ghastly experience and refused now to lie in his bed, insisting he will not sleep until he is sent home. This is the reverse of the case last year when an Indian boy climbed into his bed on the first day and refused to leave it until collected by his long-suffering mother, herself the headmistress of a very well respected school near Delhi. How I bled for her then, but now, in this new case, my sympathies are entirely with the boy.

A group of senior girls came to see me to say that a married teacher had confided in them, for some incomprehensible reason, that she had had an *affaire* with a young member of staff. They felt burdened by this unnecessary confidence, not unnaturally, and felt guilty at spilling the beans to me but also terrified of getting involved. If it's in the public domain I've obviously got to confront my colleague with this damaging state of 'affairs' while protecting the identities of the girls. Were it still an entirely private, confidential matter, given that neither teacher named is attached to a boarding house, I'd tend to ignore it. This will be tricky.

Chapter 2

Orally James has found his feet

AUGUST 1995. We are hosting the Flying Disc World Championships. Frisbees to the rest of us. There are a thousand people here for a week from the United States, Japan and almost everywhere in between. A mixed team of young men and women from the States that had not scored a point throughout the competition decide to take all their clothes off—a disconcerting move for the opposition but entirely legitimate in the specialized world of flying discs it seems—and score immediately. Is there a lesson here for school sport, I wonder?

Mr Li Shou Goa comes to see me with his son Zhang. If I understand the interpreter correctly, he is the Chairman of the Communist Party in Beijing and as such is certainly the most powerful person I have ever met, although he modestly conceals any impression of the range of his influence at our meeting. It seems that it was his father who, as the general in charge of the Beijing garrison, handed over the city without bloodshed to Mao Tse Tung's general, Deng Xiaoping, during the civil war. In gratitude, Deng adopted the Li family as his own and I am thus interviewing Deng's adopted grandson, a friendly, rather fat little boy who I suspect has been pretty indulged in his short life this far.

I take a visiting sculptress round the exhibition of Elizabeth Frink's sculptures, which have graced the campus all summer.

'All the Heads look like her; they have her chin,' she said. I ask her whether this also applies to her water buffalo.

'Less so, but a bit.'

It is rather touching, when the term is under way, to see two third-year girls sitting quietly on the grass by the eight-foot high, well endowed male nude, fashioning a sort of loin cloth for him out of evergreen branches. When I enquire why they feel this is necessary, they suggest that they thought he looked chilly. What, in mid summer? 'Well, you never know, Sir, do you?' There's no arguing with that.

The period just before the start of a new school year is like a sort of phoney war. With a fortnight to go, the maintenance staff are flat out clearing up after the summer schools and camps and preparing the campus and boarding houses for the return of the pupils. Late applicants are still being processed, tutors are starting to come in to sort out their mail and classrooms, senior colleagues are hard at it, tweaking the timetable, covering all the bases involved in preparing to welcome 380 new pupils and 14 new teachers. Most of all, they are trying to answer the steady stream of post GCSE and A-Level queries from our own and from new pupils who seek advice on what their next steps should be. And all this with not a single child in sight. Among the reading I try to cover in this busy limbo is a US high school brochure in which I read, 'All passive recreations are encouraged in school including sitting, sunning, picnicking...and academic classes.'

After the staff meetings, the sixth-form parents' meeting and the various year group assemblies, the term gets under way at last and we're surfing again. In the first couple of days I have met parents from Thailand, Japan, the Philippines, India, South Africa and England. Only the last voices a complaint—about a girl with whom his daughter is sharing a room. It reminded me of a Major, who insisted on sporting his rank, complaining to his daughter's houseparent that she was 'sharing with three foreign girls.' 'Don't worry,' my colleague apparently replied, 'I'm sure they won't mind.'

'Top School Swim Coach in Sex Scandal.' Reports in seven national papers and on HTV covering the trial of Paul Hickson, our former swimming coach for a year, are all pretty accurate as far as I can tell except that they all infer that our pupils were somehow involved or even attacked, which was not the case. Protracted attempts follow to get them to publish a disclaimer and in the case of *The Times*, *The Sun*, the *Independent* and HTV we are successful.

Mr Modi and his wife come to see me to register their gratitude for the successful conclusion of their son's first week with us. They are delightful people who own an airline ('ModiLuft—the only private one flying out of Delhi'), hospitals, schools and commercial outlets, and their base is a town bearing their name. They educate 3,000 children free of charge. Karam, who is in Orchards House, has told them with some pride that he has just made himself a cheese sandwich and poured himself a Coke—the first things he has ever had to do for himself. There are, it appears, thirty servants at home. There are none, of course, in Orchards.

James comes to see me. He is quite a demanding boy, not surprisingly perhaps, given that both his parents are dead, poor fellow, and he has been drifting for some time with dire results in his GCSEs. I have allowed him back on compassionate grounds but the term has not started well. He's a tough guy, a good rugby player, and so what he had to say really shook me.

'I spoke with my mother last night. I often have conversations with her when I need help. She's told me what to do. It's the best advice I've ever had. I'm going to take three A Levels and become a really positive pupil. You'll see.'

The conversations with his mother, he told me, are held through a medium. He seems so sure that he can make it work this time, so obviously I give him a final chance.

Talking with our Arabist, I realize for the first time, and rather late in the day, how hard it has been for Sattam Al Saud and the other Saudi princes to try to adapt to life here, where we expect from them the same level of effort that we would of anyone else. At home they have power of life and death—almost literally—over their teachers. A teacher who had the temerity to reprimand a royal pupil would be open to physical attack and the sack. No wonder poor Sattam found everything here so perplexing. A few years back, I remember, one of his cousins shot a local councillor, who happened to be passing his House as he was aiming at an air pistol target placed in the window of his room. He missed the target and hit the councillor, who was fortunately wearing a thick fur coat at the time. Otherwise the consequences might have been much worse than merely getting *The Sun* on the phone at midnight. In the light of what I have just learnt, no wonder the poor boy was so surprised that we took it all so seriously at the time.

Vinu Baig comes in from New Delhi with her daughter and son, Sheena and Rizvan, both Old Millfieldians. She is setting up the Millfield Association in India and has been indefatigable already on our behalf. It is a real pleasure to meet her at last. Her analysis of the spoilt brat syndrome in some Indian circles helps to explain why three boys who were to join us backed out at the last moment. While in my room she suddenly became worried about her brother's health, so I encouraged her to call him. She spoke for a minute or two in Hindi and then turned back to the rest of us. 'Bad news. He died two hours ago.'

This morning highlights the multi-cultural exhilaration of being a truly international school. First, Ben Tan arrives from China, full of reasons why we should visit Shanghai, where he has recently built 10,000 family homes, in order to recruit pupils. Then Mr George, a parent, shows up to try to persuade me to visit Brummana School, outside Beirut, which wants a British headteacher to introduce a British curriculum. Both are unlikely possibilities, for I am aware that in a school boasting fifty-seven nationalities among its pupils, one could spend the whole year out and about on the recruiting trail while neglecting the school itself.

Facing me in chapel today were two sixth-formers who have been much in my mind recently, the one who lost all her hair during extensive chemotherapy for leukaemia, but who never lost her optimism; and the other who was raped by a family friend during the holiday. They are two young women whose courage in adversity I could not admire more; they having known anguish on a level which has been spared me almost all of my life.

I read today about Brian MacKinnon who, at the age of 34, enrolled under an alias at his old school and spent a year there. Apparently no one at the school checked or even guessed his age or, astonishingly, even recognized him from the five years he'd spent there. It occurs to me that independent schools need lots of Brians if they are to stay full in these competitive times.

I am hobbling around with one black shoe and one white trainer, having broken my foot. Any claim to gravitas is up the creek. A third-year boy surveys the wreckage of my footwear, enquires politely how I am and asks perceptively, 'Do you have another pair like that at home, Sir?' Later, as I pass two strapping third-year girls in conversation, a diminutive boy hurries past on his way to games. The girls watch with interest, then turn to each other and say in chorus, 'How sweet.' Thank God he didn't hear this.

At an advisory board meeting of the Teacher Training Agency, a spokesman from the Department for Education and Employment declares that 'the data on teacher recruitment is being cleaned.' This sounds ominous, but not as ominous as the news later in the meeting that the three main target areas to try to tackle the chronic shortage of recruits for the profession are the handicapped, ethnic minorities—and men. Anthea Millett is our chairman. I have always admired her, ever since she once talked about 'the irritating success of wrong methods.'

Today feels like the worst day of the term so far. 'Top School ignored Swim Coach Warning.' The whole front page of *Today* is covered with it. Only one family in the school had known Paul

Hickson in his previous existence at Swansea, when he doubled as a GB Olympic swimming coach. They had specifically chosen to send their daughter to us when Paul arrived last year as our coach, so that he could continue as her trainer. They now accuse us of not knowing about his past, though they were themselves in a better position than anyone to know about this. Now that their daughter will not be called as a witness because her statement is so weak, her family have tried to get their own back with a paid deal from *Today*.

The rest of the day is spent on the phone with the Chairman of Governors, the school solicitor, a public relations friend in London, whom I used to teach, the police officer in charge of the case, the Crown Prosecution Service and the Press Complaints Board. I call a cabinet meeting to discuss the matter, write a long press statement and fax it to all the national dailies, write a letter to all governors and parents, tell the staff what's going on and, in the middle of all this mayhem, teach a General Studies lesson—a calming oasis of reality. Happily, my conscience on the matter is entirely clear. Had I feared that I *might* at any stage have disregarded a suggestion of sexual impropriety concerning our swimming coach, I would know all about it inside. The only silver lining to this black cloud is the fact that *Today* goes out of business a week later. Nemesis appears to be on our side.

It is incredible that this same day should be the day of the trial of a peripatetic member of the music staff, charged with, and subsequently cleared of, indecency years ago with private pupils outside the school. Peripatetic instrumental teachers are in some jeopardy, for the bulk of their lessons are given to individual pupils and instruction often requires a certain amount of close work with the pupil, correcting anything from grip to embouchure. This man is above reproach but the charges have taken a heavy toll on him and his family. Two papers made the connection with our swimming coach, though.

Today Hung-Jong Lee, newly arrived from Korea, who speaks almost no English but who after only one month is already deeply popular here, plays his clarinet in chapel and is rewarded by an entirely spontaneous round of applause. It is extraordinary to see him later in the week singing in his House choir in the House song competition—extraordinary only because it was the Anvil Chorus from *Il Trovatore* and because they sang it in Italian. The following day, the crowd watching our 1st XV doing battle with Llandovery suddenly launch themselves into the Chorus again, word perfect and in harmony. It must have shaken our visitors more than a little, especially when it's normally the Welsh with whom one associates passionate community singing.

At the Headmasters' Conference annual meeting in Dublin, Brendan Kennelly, Professor of Modern Literature at Trinity College, spoke for an hour without notes, moving effortlessly in and out of prose and poetry as he worked his magic on us. He told the story of Brendan Behan who, when asked the difference between poetry and prose, replied:

> There was a young fellah named Rollocks
> Who worked for Ferrier Pollocks.
> As he walked on the Strand
> With his girl by the hand
> The tide came up to his knees.
> Now that's prose. If the tide had been in, it would have
> been poetry.

With a day to go to half-term, I find myself, at 6.45, ending my nineteenth consecutive meeting, the first of which started at 7.30 in the morning with our counsellor and a houseparent who came to talk of the events of the night before. These had been disturbing. In the teeth of an onslaught from her drunken and abusive mother, a day girl had decided to stay with her friend locally instead of returning home. The business was complicated by the fact that she had tested their friendship over a period by perpetrating a number of plainly disgusting acts in her presence, embarrassing the girlfriend and her family. These were matters which her mother refused to face up to. We at school were cast in the role of go-between—going between the girl, her mother and the innocent but outraged family of the friend. There are times when even the Israel–Palestine problem seems susceptible to a quicker remedy than the average 14-year-old's emotional turmoil.

This is just one example of what we are coming to see as a greatly increased pastoral workload this term for house staff. Why is this? None of us really know. It's not just the familiar 'I'm paying you to look after them' syndrome. It may be a reflection of the very different backgrounds from which our people come, with their correspondingly different expectations, but then that has always obtained at Millfield.

It all seems to have started with the father who came to see me after his 13-year-old son had been with us for less than a week.

'There is no criticism of the school, or the House, or the other pupils,' he assured me, 'It's just that when I left him here the day before term started, I did not like the look of the other parents.'

And he removed his son from the context in which the poor boy had just established himself on what appeared to be nothing but a bizarre whim. There are just more unreasonable parents about these days, it seems, who demand so much more of the staff's emotional energy than they deserve.

As if to exemplify this, a senior member of the preparatory school's staff writes to say he will be away on sick leave for a while. 'Edgarley is a contact sport,' he adds, by way, I suppose, of an explanation.

The penalty for taking three days off over half-term is that 132 letters addressed to me await me on my return.

Dick Snelling died yesterday aged seventy. He taught some twenty languages here for over thirty years. I saw his timetable when I first arrived. Monday 1st period: classical Greek, Swahili,

Mandarin and Portuguese, all at the same time, to individual pupils, moving between them in a personalized, systematic procedure that ensured everyone was working all the time. But he was really an anthropologist who was still teaching with undiminished gusto right to the end of his life. His pupils and colleagues are devastated. Perhaps the key to his unequalled success was that he was still so clearly learning all the time. He must be the last of the best of Jack Meyer's eccentric scholars. We are going to put a bench up for him on the cricket boundary where he used to like to sit, and at his request it will bear the inscription: 'There is some corner of an English field that is forever foreign.'

Today I enjoyed the pleasure of the company of the Yuvraj, son of the Maharaja of Dhrangadhra, one of Millfield's first pupils, who looked in on his way home to India. This pleasure is, however, quickly dispelled by a man who wants to set up a Masonic lodge based on the school. All my hackles go up even in places where I did not know I had places, let alone hackles. He finds it hard to take no as an answer, assuming, I think, that I will cave in if he just drones on and on. Getting him to leave is hard; he's a lot bigger than I am.

I was visiting Kevin Cheney at his prep school at Cranmore and remarked on the beautiful setting and condition of his cricket pitch. 'Ah, that's Norman,' said Kevin. It was several seconds, as I wrestled in my mind with a distant doubt that cricket after all might have been French before it became English, before I realized he was talking about his groundsman.

A third-year boy went jogging round Street yesterday and miraculously got lost, so he knocked on a door and asked for help. 'Is there anyone I can ring for you who might help?' said the kind householder in surprise.

'You could try my mother,' said the boy. Ten minutes later, a tutor in the staff room is called to the phone.

'My son is lost in Street. Do you know where he is?'

'No,' replied the tutor, 'Could you tell me who your son is and where you are speaking from?'

'His name is James and I'm speaking from Chicago,' came the reply.

Last night Kate, a fifth-form girl, was walking back to her House across the campus from a play rehearsal. It was about 9.30 and she was alone, but all the lights were on and she, being on home territory, was entirely unprepared for what then happened. Without warning two men, either high on drugs or drink, appeared from nowhere and attacked her, forcing her to the ground and trying to carry her off. Kate is strong and must have fought back with all her very considerable spirit. Her screams attracted Duncan, our duty security man. His arrival put the men to flight and they disappeared into the campus. Duncan assured himself that Kate was not seriously hurt before trying to see where the men had got to. He soon came across an unfamiliar red van with the keys conveniently still in the ignition, so he removed them and waited to see what transpired. After a while, the men returned, whereupon Duncan seems to have managed to lock them in their van and then helped the police arrest them.

It only transpired later that one of them was wanted on a murder charge and that they might have been trying to abduct Kate rather than merely attack her. But for Duncan's rapid response and quick-witted action we might have been faced with real tragedy. Kate will need all the support we can corporately offer her to get through this. Duncan deserves a medal.

After a bewildering day's course at Bromsgrove School on the 'Superhighway', it is chastening to recall the Western Union Telegraph's reply to Alexander Bell when he proposed his telephone: 'After careful consideration of your invention, while it is a very interesting novelty, we have come to the conclusion that it has no commercial possibilities.'

An unforgettable Saturday. Dr James Watson, he of the double helix with Crick, visited Millfield to talk to the sixth-form. The theatre was crammed with well over 600 people—thankfully no Health and Safety spies visited at the time. After lunch with the pupils, he had a game of tennis with our coach. As he was leaving, one of our pupils asked him if it wasn't an anticlimax getting a Nobel Prize at age twenty-five.

'What did you do next?'

'I got a girlfriend.'

Tonight the Show Choir concluded Stephen Pinnock's first school concert since his arrival as Director of Music this term. There were 140 of them, impeccable in their white shirts and black skirts and trousers and they sang their hearts out to an enthusiastic audience. It's the final outcome of the need for a new approach, a vindication of the anguish generated since before Stephen's appointment by the whole saga of involving as many pupils as possible in music. For the first time, music is starting to touch the heart of the school, and will, I hope, no longer be the preserve of just the very highly gifted exponents. One rough and tough member of the choir who is also in the 1st XV told me afterwards with characteristic brevity that it was 'the best experience I've had with my clothes on, Sir.' Later, after a most successful school concert at which nevertheless there was a smaller number of pupils listening than participating, I asked the whole orchestra and choir to perform again one Saturday in one of our gyms. The whole school was required to attend. At lunch I was astonished to realize how very few of the younger pupils had ever heard an orchestra in the flesh before.

Following the Watson lecture, I receive an irate letter from a parent of a boy in the lower school. 'I gather a Nobel Prize winner came to speak last week. My son was not able to attend, presumably because he is too thick. Whatever the reason, it is shameful.' Given that not even the whole sixth-form could squeeze in to hear Dr Watson, let alone the lower school, what is shameful is the vocabulary and logic of this parent. The fact that he is a QC does nothing to increase one's respect for the legal profession.

The Nick Bollettieri tennis experiment is not an unmitigated success. The imported American coach is a pleasant enough chap but has gone from spaced out to manic in the space of twenty-four hours. Players are disgruntled and even our loyal assistant coaches are far from gruntled. And it is now clear that he is drinking. So the top Spanish coach on the Bollettieri circuit will come next week for a fortnight in an attempt to rescue the situation and our coaches will be flown to Florida at Christmas for a crash course. I hope this works, for we risk losing our three best players otherwise. Thus a meeting this morning at 9.0 with Martin van Toll (Becker's sparring partner and subsequently chief coach here), and the Bollettieri European manager to try to iron out all the wrinkles.

HMC Committee for two days at Fishmongers Hall. The result of the election for next year's chairman is announced and it is not going to be me. Apparently it took three recounts and at the end just a handful of votes separated the three of us. At least that is what I am told, but perhaps that's just a gentle way of letting me down. But Michael Mavor at Rugby is successful and Patrick Tobin and I languish. People are very kind but it is a blow, there's no disguising that.

Today must rank high among the sort of days Heads dread. Just a day after the exhilaration of *Guys and Dolls*, the Christmas Ball produces eight drunk girls. For three years this has been a wonderfully trouble-free event, with around 300 young people, all dressed to kill, enjoying a superb event in complete safety, perhaps—given the excesses awaiting them at universities—for the last time in their lives. But now, out of the blue, people with unblemished records have let themselves and us down badly and must be suspended. There are tears all over the carpet. Then, for the first time in my five years here, there's a report from the school doctor to let me know that two third-formers have been to see him to say that they have had intercourse. The girl requests and is given the morning-after pill. It is a tough decision for our wise and experienced doctor who, of course, cannot tell me the pupils' names. And finally, just when you think things cannot get much worse, there's the news that a visiting soccer side's changing room has been ransacked with theft and gratuitous vandalism. The fall-out from each of these affairs will be enormous and will keep a number of senior staff busy for hours, if not days. What a way to embark on the last week of term!

At 7 a.m. I am off to a meeting with the counsellor and the doctor about the two 13-year-olds having sex when opposite the pool a taxi draws up and four bleary-eyed boys from Etonhurst, a House some three miles away, spill out.

'We've come for recreational swimming, Sir. Our first time.'

'What, now?'

'Yes, Sir, look, it says so here: 6 to 8.' Only then did they realize it meant p.m., not a.m. However, when the elite swimmers, who of course had been at it for an hour already, began to appreciate the enormity of the sacrifice made by these poor blighters, they kindly squeezed up and made a spare lane for them, so virtue was rewarded after all.

The last day of term, the one we all reach by the skin of our teeth with enough emotional energy in reserve to see us through until the evening, with luck. It is made by the splendid service in Wells Cathedral, which we fill, and by the upbeat mood of the various assemblies. It is marred, however, by the news that a married assistant in a boarding house is now known to be having an *affaire* with another member of staff, and also by the fact that our 13-year-old, contrary to advice from the doctor, has today told others about her sexual encounter and her name is widely known. This means that I must ask my colleague to leave the boarding house and the poor pupil to leave the school. No boarding school can afford to keep any youngster when it is common knowledge among either pupils or staff—in this case both—that he or she has had sex on campus. Being the biggest co-educational boarding school in the country makes us statistically the more vulnerable to such eventualities, and it astonishes me therefore that this is the first such case I have encountered here. The irony is that, as yet, no one is aware of the boy's name, except of course the school doctor, and thus no comparable action can be taken against him, whoever he is. The fact that the girl has not divulged his identity is greatly to her credit. I will do everything I can to ensure that she finds a good second home elsewhere.

The next day we say goodbye to Don, our tennis coach, who is poured into a taxi to Heathrow and, if he makes it, a plane back to Florida. Even at this twelfth hour he is skating, or given his alcohol intake, sloshing around the main issues. Martin, his successor, does seem to have a much better idea of how we now need to progress things, so our experiment with Bollettieri is given a restorative kiss of life.

Now we move into that unnerving and unwelcome limbo when the young have deserted the campus, rendering it sterile, and yet the term still needs to be polished off. There are 1,250 reports to be written before one can start to unwind a bit. I take heart from whatever contacts with the young come my way, vicariously today from the published extract from a Bristol Cathedral chorister's diary, illustrating the importance of fresh views on history: 'We were shown a plaque of Captain Scott who got lost on a trip to the South Pole.'

Reports are finished. I must have written 20,000 words. Will any of them help anyone in their studies or their wider development? The level of interest in and knowledge of the young is high among nearly all tutors, and for the main part their reports illustrate this again and again, yet some persist in writing clichés which could apply to almost anyone, young or old. 'Could do better' is for me the nadir of unhelpful comment. Of which of us could that not be said? My acid test as a teacher is to re-read each class's reports when I've written them, without looking at the names. If I cannot attribute a report to the right pupil, then it needs to be done again. But as headmaster there is no chance of this, except perhaps in the senior year. If, on average, every report contains twelve report slips, and given that they are written in triplicate, there are some 45,000 report slips to be handled twice a year, a massive logistical operation, managed impeccably by the whole office staff in unison. I only recall so far one error being drawn to our attention. This involved two boys in the fourth-year with the same first and last names, though with different middle initials. One report was misattributed, and resulted, understandably perhaps, in a letter of censure from the parent concerned.

I recall as a housemaster at Westminster going through his report with a particular boy, Robert Rosenthal.

'You seem to be making good progress in Art.'

'But Sir, I don't do Art.'

'Ah,' say I, coughing to hide my embarrassment for my elderly art colleague. The next term at the comparable meeting Robert prompted me encouragingly.

'How am I getting on in Art, Sir?'

I had to confess that his report suggested he was still making good progress. You could not get away with that sort of thing these days.

This term my favourite reports are: 'Orally, he has found his feet', 'He has worked steadily, though his work is erratic' and 'His powers of concentration are not quite up to keeping all his balls in the air at once.'

Chapter 3

Defamatory comments remain unexplained

JANUARY 1996. A mother comes to see me to explain that she wants to remove her son after just one term. She insists that she has nothing but admiration for all that we have done for her boy already, but it turns out that he has always wanted to go to Eton, and has rightly deduced that we are not it. She says he feels different from the other pupils here, but I wonder how he can feel more 'different' than, say, those who come from fifty-four different countries to be here, and who make the most of their difference. Anyway, her mind is made up and she will take him tomorrow to Sherborne where she hopes that he will feel less 'different'. But what a terrible shame it is that he should flee difference when we should all revel in it. Is this our fault? His? I am really depressed by this interview. The Brassens song that I have introduced to countless classes in my time springs to mind: 'les braves gens n'aiment pas que l'on suive une autre route qu'eux.' Vive la différence!

Monsieur Braconnier rings from New York, the first contact from him in three months. He has done so because, most reluctantly, I have had to talk to Marie, the eldest of his three elegant daughters, to alert her to the fact that her father will not answer letters or the phone, will not pay the fees, and is thus now jeopardising the girls' future here. I tell him that they may not return tomorrow until last term's fees have been settled. He tells me all his money is now wrapped up in pharmaceuticals. 'Le contrat que j'ai attendu est bloqué jusqu'à fin janvier.' I have to stand my ground though I am as aware as he is of the devastating effect this will have on the girls who are wonderfully embedded in the full life of the school.

The first day of term and I take three different Assemblies with the year groups in succession. They never get any easier. I am always nervous and hate using notes in case, while I'm looking down at them, all the pupils do a bunk. So I am in my room at 7.15 reworking what I want to say, and settle on lukewarmness as the main danger which might confront us in this still fairly new year. I take a poem by Spike Milligan and the passage from St Luke on the Laodiceans by way of illustrations. In the event the third-years and fourth-years are either too sleepy or too self-conscious to laugh at my jokes. Or maybe the jokes are just not funny. But the sixth-formers, it sounds like all 600 of them, are cheeringly responsive and yet still observe punctiliously the full minute's silence I have introduced with which to end the Assembly, a practice I have swiped from Hereford Cathedral School. Anyone could wreck it in any one of a thousand ways, but none of them do. My nerves are worth it, though will any of them remember anything I've said by lunchtime? Actually, unusually, one boy does mention it later in the afternoon.

'I enjoyed what you said this morning, Sir, but I couldn't understand much of it.'

Well, who knows? Perhaps that's better than the other way round.

At the end of the first week I check to see with how many of the staff I have managed to have some sort of personal exchange since the holiday, and I count 121, meaning I have failed so far with 70 others. It's rather a contrived exercise perhaps, but I feel

I must try to develop some sort of system for this, rather than leaving it all to casual encounters. I've been to the library, the tuck shop, the carpentry shop, the kitchens, the school shop and a variety of games and activities sessions. I've toured two sets of parents, hung around in breaks to talk to pupils and held all the usual meetings. Yet despite all this, I feel for the first time a sense of distance from the school, which I can only hope is transitory. Is this age? Or am I conscious now as never before of retirement in two years' time?

Recruitment has been a problem for many schools for some years now and we are just beginning to feel the pinch ourselves, with lower third-form entries than ever before. This is compensated by increased numbers of fourth-form and sixth-form entries, but I can see why some Heads practically sleep with the entries file under their pillow. No particular pattern seems to emerge here and the future looks difficult to predict in at least six ways; numbers of entries, the ages of entry, girl as opposed to boy entries, the quality of entries, the timing of entries, which get later every year, and the cost of fee concessions. And is our reputation for our work with dyslexic children now working to our disadvantage with parents of such children applying earlier and in increasing numbers, threatening to some extent the balance in the school?

It becomes clear at an Executive meeting that we will now have to write a strategic plan. The timing is right, I must concede, but I do not relish the thought at all. I have always seen schools, and especially this one, as organic organisations, responding to changing circumstances as flexibly as possible, to benefit today's as opposed to yesterday's youngsters. I have in the past seen a five-year plan as a strait jacket, but must now learn to see it as an adaptable tool for measuring our success against agreed targets. And more importantly, I must try to get my colleagues to regard it in the same light; not a piece of cake, though some, I have no doubt, are more enlightened on this score than I am.

I asked a boy about his holidays today and he replied with unconscious irony, 'Oh, great, Sir. My parents are divorcing so I got two holidays.'

Julia and I toured Etonhurst last night with Sam, the Head of House. He looks fifteen, is fresh-faced, without guile and is no games player. You would not assume he would cut much ice with the other boys but he clearly has great respect throughout the House. There is silence in prep long before ever we appear on the scene. How does he do it? 'Well I don't really know Sir. They're all so nice.' It strikes me as a good cameo of how liking people seems so often to get the best out of them.

A sad week. I have to expel two people for cannabis possession and immediately there are twenty press enquiries. The same day, I write personally to every national paper's education correspondent with news and photographs of our six tutors who are the first to complete our own internally devised M. Ed. course, validated by the University of the West of England. As far as I know, this is a first in the country, and a major move along the trail of continuous professional development for teachers. No one publishes any reference to this at all, not even the *TES*, but the *Daily Express* gives our two expelled pupils three columns. I am bitterly disappointed, but I must be naive to be surprised. I do know, after all, that for journalists, bad news is good news and good news is no news. The press are relaxed with the cliché that Millfield is nothing but a sports school. They do not like to have to come to terms with anything more complicated, such as the fact that we are a serious academic institution. But when you thumb through the tabloids, and recall that they represent the only print that very many people ever read, is it so surprising that the UK seems to come bottom of so many international league tables?

Wednesday afternoon is games afternoon. The sun came out, and with it a sense of optimism. I don't think I saw one glum face all afternoon. I watched some tennis, fencing, judo, squash, climbing, weight-training, badminton, riding, aerobics and an U14 girls' hockey match. Our coach, whose Irish humour never deserts her, was shouting our girls on from the touchline.

'Oh, unlucky,' she calls as the ball is driven past our goalkeeper to give the opposition a lead. Then *sotto voce* to me, 'It's bad play really but you have to encourage them or they cry.' Leaning over the railing watching them, one mother said unprompted by me, 'My daughter's nicer since she came here. She's more considerate. That's what boarding does for you, I suppose.'

Rachel, who has just joined us from Taiwan, still has trouble with her genders and pronouns. Apparently she has told her tutor Group, 'I'm not sleeping well. My roommate, he keep me awake all night.'

At the Junior hop, run by one of the girls' Houses, there is the usual racket, war-paint, miniskirts, too many bare midriffs, flashing lights, dry ice and ear-splitting music. They all seem to be having a ball. Bellowing into my ear as we watch from the sidelines, a senior girl on duty shrieks, 'I'm so glad I'm not young any more, Sir.'

Visiting Southfields House, we encounter in one room a girl who lives in Minehead and who has never been abroad—and nor, it transpires, has her father—sharing with Evgenia Raspopina who comes three times a year to Street to study here and who lives in Vladivostock. I cannot think off-hand of any boarders who live respectively closer or further away than they do.

The French play is *Un ami imprévu* which turns out to be a version of *The Mousetrap*. The native French speakers are good, of course, but some of the others, while confident, are almost incomprehensible. At the curtain call an enthusiastic audience reserves its biggest round of applause for Ed Finlay, killed in his wheelchair early on before being required to utter a single word.

Father Aidan, an admirable Franciscan friar, talked in chapel today about his three vows. Poverty, 'I own nothing, not even my sandals or my underwear'; Chastity, 'A tough one, much to the girls' disappointment'; and Obedience, 'If anyone needs what I have more than I do, I must give it to him.' The pupils are mesmerized. Some, I suspect, who are more than others victims of the post-Thatcherite mind-set, simply cannot believe him. Afterwards, with those who stayed behind to talk, he refers to his isolation for two years in the Australian desert, of his loneliness as a chaplain with Missions to Seamen and of his alcoholism ('I was on one-and-a-half litres of whisky a day').

The impact he undoubtedly has on the youngsters around him seems to stem from this magic mixture of his religious conviction and devotion on the one side, and of his flawed humanity, just like the rest of us, on the other. He is the sort of person you just don't forget.

Half-term week is a week's recruiting in India, starting with arrival at 1.30 a.m. at Delhi to a welcome arranged by Mr Modi (he of the airline) with flower garlands, a limo—the works. We stayed with Abbas Ali Baig, one of India's great cricketing heroes, and his wife Vinu. They are wonderfully hospitable and sociable and within hours of our arrival they whisked us off to the British High Commission for a reception for what seemed like the entire diplomatic corps. Standing on the lawns under the fairy lights, I am approached by someone claiming we have met somewhere before. We both furrowed our brows and wracked our brains until eventually it dawned on us both simultaneously where this might be. The link we had in common was his daughter, who was one of those I expelled for cannabis last month. We both quite enjoyed the awkwardness of the situation. He accepted the position in a most civilized way and I welcomed his company. I was horrified to learn in due course that barely a month later he had died on a ski slope.

We took the Shatabdi Express up to Dehradun to establish a school exchange with Millfield at the Doon School. Lunch was memorable for my introduction to the legendary and unforgettably named General Bakshee. He is more English, and more military, than the most military of Englishmen. I enquired about his wife: where was she? The reply exceeded all my expectations. 'She's in Poona.'

The two admirable boys who will be our first exchange pupils at Millfield took me round this elegant school where the impeccable manners of teachers and boys alike would be almost anachronistic in the UK. The afternoon train had us back in Delhi station, still teeming with countless thousands of people, at midnight. Then into the maelstrom of traffic, where a million taxis and auto-rickshaws vie for what available space they can find, the latter optimistically sporting slogans telling everyone else how to drive; 'Keep Distance', 'Give Side' and 'Please Horn'. Only the last of these seems to get any positive response from fellow competitors.

Among the various prospective parents and pupils we met in Delhi was Kohelika Kohli who rides for India, and who will in due course so excel herself at Millfield that she will become Head of School. She came with her mother Sunita, who designed the Prime Minister's office. Building these Indian links has particular importance for us at Millfield, for the first six pupils brought over at our foundation in 1935 by Jack Meyer were all the sons of maharajas whom he had met here. Our roots lie as much here as they do in Somerset.

Waiting with Vinu and her son Rizvan at Delhi airport to fly down to Mumbai, I bought a copy of Salman Rushdie's *The Moor's Last Sigh*. Sitting between them during our flight, it was weird to read the chapter devoted to the 'Kissing of Abbas Ali Baig', her husband and his father respectively. He played cricket for India and in 1960 helped his team salvage a draw against Australia with a second half-century. This prompted an anonymous sari-clad Hindu girl to rush onto the pitch and spontaneously greet him, a Muslim, with an admiring (and scandalously public) kiss. But it was weirder still to find ourselves having supper that night in Farida's house, which had been Rushdie's own home, and which features so prominently in the early part of *Midnight's Children*.

[39]

From 34° in Mumbai to -10° at Heathrow. Snow cornices by the road on the way back. I got to school at 5 p.m., just in time to accept an HMI oral report on their inspection. They were completely won over by the pupils. One said it was the best atmosphere in any school she had visited. A very welcome endorsement indeed. They have understood that Millfield has something unique. We all know it, but it is tantalisingly difficult to isolate the contributing factors. Later, as jet lag started to bite, I accept a call from the Yeovil Conservative Women's Association. They want me to talk at one of their meetings.

'We'll give a donation to any charity you like to name,' added their secretary.

'The Lib Dems,' I suggested helpfully. Luckily, she laughed.

Simon Armitage, with others including Christopher Booker and Gillian Clarke, spoke at our sixth-form Literature Conference. He read his poetry and explained that once, when at school, his headmaster had summoned him to remonstrate with him over something he had written in the school magazine.

'In our school,' he apparently argued, 'We don't like poetry that has language in it.'

Impossibly confrontational parents wrote today asking me to admit their long-suffering son as a boarder next term. This far he has been a day boy and while his teachers admire his efforts, we have almost all found it hard to cope with the steady stream of criticism and invective from his parents. I replied that I should need some sort of guarantee of their general support before wishing them on any boarding houseparents. A furious fax from them then lands on my desk. 'We demand an immediate meeting... You will explain your defamatory comments.' Is it possible that they actually do not know how universally they are regarded, among experienced teachers, as a real pain? I will probably end up offering the poor chap a place on compassionate grounds, if only to spare him from his parents.

Four times a week, prospective parents visit me in small groups to grill me on Millfield and my views on everything from compulsory games to bulimia. Today, however, there was a variation on the theme, which I enjoyed. 'Headmaster, what is your stance on sex?' In my reply, I hope I succeeded in giving satisfaction.

I was cheered to hear today that the Wali of Swat, in Pakistan, had been in touch about his dyslexic son's possible entry. There is unseemly speculation in the Admissions Office as to what the son of a Wali could be called, especially one from Swat. This was only interrupted by the arrival of the next British Ambassador to a Middle Eastern fiefdom. He has two daughters here and wanted to talk about their future. During our conversation it turned out that only yesterday he had kissed hands with the Queen on his appointment. She had asked him what he thought of the Arab peoples with whom he had previously worked. His reply was no doubt diplomatic, but he had apparently added that he thought that they were often prone to make quick, unexpected decisions.

'Just like my daughters-in-law! Those two!' she had replied with asperity.

In a single day, four desperate cases of children's distress are reported to me. First there's an anorexic girl who has gone from eleven to seven stone in weight since the summer. She exercises excessively, swimming three times a day, and refuses to co-operate with the school doctor in his attempts to implement a recovery, let alone stabilize her weight loss. Her mother refuses to acknowledge that there is a problem and has now disappeared to Tokyo. Another girl has been self-harming. Her mother died when she was young and her father has now wisely decided to remove her to have her close to him as a day pupil. As if this was not all bad enough, a boy still in his first year, whose grandfather admits to beating him with a horsewhip on the family estate in Ireland, has just stolen a purse, the culmination of a long list of other offences. I cannot suspend him, for he will be attacked again at home, so we must all try to elicit understanding for him among his peers, who are losing patience with him. Finally, I learn of the plight of a girl whose father, some years ago, slashed her mother's throat, and was recently released from prison. He has tried to make contact with the girl, leaving messages for her at her House. The CID are in touch, anxious both for the girl and for her mother, who has police protection. The local police have been informed but all this places an enormous burden of care on her houseparents. If you were devising case studies for a course for new Heads you would probably not include these for fear that they would be thought too extreme.

I drive three colleagues up to visit Kevin Satchwell in his City Technology College at Telford. It is a most instructive and stimulating day and we realize immediately that we are looking at something special from which we have a lot to learn. The technological initiatives are impressive by any standard, as is Paul, their research centre boss, who is clearly a workaholic. He logs on from home and carries on his work on the school's systems there in the evenings. 'The only difference between work and leisure is that in leisure you make your own coffee.' It is no surprise in due course to hear that Kevin has been knighted for his incomparable services to education.

Yad Vashem has been in the news so I decide to do an assembly on it, quoting one chilling letter from a young officer working at the railhead to Auschwitz to his commander, which I remember seeing in that astonishing building. In it, he writes that the number of Jews passing through has increased so much that his men are at full stretch—either fewer Jews or more troops are needed. I add that I have always assumed that, had I been born ten years earlier in Germany, I would have joined the Hitler Jugend, for that was where my friends would have been and I would not have had the nerve to be left out. This arouses more comment subsequently than almost any assembly I've ever taken, with most people apparently pleased by my honesty.

We are looking for a librarian so I study the trade paper regularly for hints about the range of jobs currently on offer. My attention is particularly drawn to an advertisement for an assistant librarian at Eton with whom we will not in this case be in competition: 'Good knowledge of Latin and Greek essential.'

People have started smoking in the dining room loos again, so we close them for a while. I am now worried that the trickle of pupils going down to the woods in break are not going there for a smoke but for a pee.

Giles Mount broke his finger playing hockey against Sherborne this afternoon and a kindly Sherborne housemaster took him to hospital for a painful operation. The nurse apparently told him he could swear if he wanted to.

'Oh, I couldn't do that,' said Giles, 'I couldn't let Millfield down.'

Bruising is seen on a girl's arm while she is swimming in the pool including what look like fingermarks. She is an athletic, courageous girl with a penchant for taking physical risks, but this cannot be overlooked and a responsible member of the PE staff reports it. The girl is adamant in her explanation, namely that she fell and a car ran over it. Her housemistress, very reasonably, now puts one or two previous incidents together in her mind, for the girl has twice returned from holiday with a broken arm and twice with bruising, always with a compelling explanation. More compelling than she offers this time, anyway. We all feel there is sufficient prima-facie evidence to justify going through our procedures, informing parents and social services. I would never have guessed at this stage how adversarial and indeed vitriolic the family would become. Far from working with us to help us understand the truth of the situation, they immediately go on the offensive. It all dragged on, even involving solicitors, and ended inconclusively, as perhaps these things are so often doomed to do.

A very welcome visit from Paul Kennedy, his wife and two daughters. I have not seen him since we worked together at Bristol Cathedral School. The visit turns out to be the idea of Mark Knopfler, he of the incomparable Dire Straits. His two sons are entering the prep school and he wants to enable their cousins, these two fine girls, to be educated in the same outfit.

A wondrous letter from the excellent Omar whom I have just asked to become a school prefect, full of intriguing literary flourishes and concluding 'I am filled with gratitude for my appointment which I graciously accept.'

The Dunblane massacre of the innocents. Unspeakable horror. A parent writes from the Middle East, initially expressing shock at the waste of young life, and my heart rises to meet him. He then continues, 'Please let me know by return what measures you are taking to ensure that a similar catastrophe cannot occur at Millfield.' He has been here. He has seen the school. He knows that our perimeter is over a mile long. He must know that, short of doubling the fees and turning the school into a fortress, such a guarantee is as likely as it is that mental illness can be abolished overnight.

This year, the Easter tour of the Far East starts with Jakarta, on the day after term ends. The hour immediately after our arrival is spent at a large reception for some fifty interested people, at which, after nearly two days without sleep, I almost certainly make even less sense than usual. But the video seems to go down well. By the next day, both my eyes are pointing in roughly the same direction again, and I meet Saleh Heinkel, the precocious but impeccably mannered son of Egyptian and German parents, who has therefore two first languages. His father is the only person I have met who has studied the details of every independent school in the UK: there's Teutonic thoroughness for you. I ask Saleh, who is twelve, about his friends.

'To the best of my knowledge,' he replies, 'Harry is my friend, because he shares my interests. I am interested primarily in what makes things work, but I am also concentrating on aircraft in the Second World War.'

This is the chap who has tamed a lizard. He's the sort of kid who, if he survives his school days, could well win a Nobel Prize, even though he may fail all his exams. But surviving his school days is the first hurdle and he will not clear it easily, I fear. It is painfully obvious that he is already more at home with adults than with his contemporaries.

I saw seven Indonesian families that morning between 8 and 2, all of whom brightened my day by their obvious enthusiasm for the multi-cultural features of Millfield. That afternoon, on the way to the airport in the back of one family's long Mercedes, I learnt that the Indonesian airline Garuda is understood locally to mean 'Go And Relax Until Delay Announced.' All this cultural information must come in useful sometime.

The Brunei reception for the Old Millfieldians is memorable this time for the absence of karaoke. This is a great relief, for most of the families there have their own karaoke sets and practise constantly, there being little else to do in Brunei, in the privacy of their homes. So no wonder Julia and I were more or less given *nul points* on all our previous visits. But now here we are in a new venue, the Royal Brunei Polo Club, as guests of Pengiran Bahrin, the Minister for Law, and his wife Masni, who, with two other former pupils, now both cabinet ministers, are the linch-pins of the Millfield Association in Brunei. The Polo Club was conceived on a scale which brings the best of Roman imperialism up to date: columns, fountains, huge double doors, attendants everywhere, yes, but also glass squash courts and a ten-pin bowling alley complete with rows of chandeliers. After the dinner, Bahrin, Masni and their son Izam showed us the three floodlit polo pitches and the 600 polo ponies—fortunately not individually—and then took us off to Jerudong Park, the vast theme park given by the Sultan to his people. By now it was well after midnight but our arrival still attracted a good deal of interest from the crowds and we found ourselves being toured around in two golf buggies driven by the manager and the chief technician. We zoomed up a 100 metre tower, hurtled around upside down on the Boomerang, and had our imaginations and our giblets stretched in the simulators. I asked the manager if there were a budget to run the park.

'Not particularly', he replied evasively and reading between the lines, I saw the blank cheque available to him. Entry is free, as are all the rides.

A day in Kuala Lumpur with the annual dinner and various interviews, including one with Arul Suppiah, a charming 13-year-old Malaysian boy who is already regarded by the Lord's ground staff as one of the most exciting young cricketers they have seen. We also had a meal with Ayman Aziz and his wife Zeti, who is the first woman Finance Director of the Bank of Negara, and whose son Alif is already at our prep school, Edgarley. Both boys are due to join us this year. It would be hard to think of two more dissimilar backgrounds than those from which they come: Alif's grandfather was the first Malay Vice-Chancellor of the University of Malaya, while Arul's parents have more modest intellectual pretensions and will depend heavily on his locally sponsored sports award. Both families are a real delight to meet.

Awaiting the plane to Hanoi, we overheard a glorious suggestion by a waiter to a customer who just could not make up his mind whether he wanted tea or coffee. 'I could bring you a mixture, Sir.' Once in Hanoi, having negotiated the chaotic but good-tempered crowds of cycles and motorbikes in the centre of town, we eventually found our hotel and embarked on a number of school visits, culminating with the Hanoi-Amsterdam school. The headmaster is immensely impressive. Here he is, running one of the biggest and certainly the most selective school in town, and clearly offering teaching which tests even these very bright youngsters, and yet he is operating on just two floors of a featureless concrete block, with huge classes and precious few resources. He himself lives with his mother in one room, cooks on a Gaz stove in the open corridor, comes to school on a bike and earns almost nothing. His commitment to his pupils is absolute; he exudes a genuine and affectionate regard for them individually. For me he epitomizes the reason why the Viet Cong could not be crushed.

Later that evening the Deputy Head brought his son Cuong and his father to see me; three generations of Vietnamese, whose respective second languages reflect the various layers of colonial attachments to their country like a sort of linguistic archaeology. But sitting round late at night talking French to the grandfather, unsteady Russian to the father and English to the son, I sensed in them no feeling of resentment or bitterness that their country had been singled out for such international banditry. Cuong is a very bright chap and we will give him a top scholarship. (Subsequently, Balliol College did the same thing to enable him to read Mathematics at Oxford.) Two pretty girls will also join us next year. One turns out to be twenty-one; her boyfriend will run her small restaurant here in her absence at Millfield as she studies for her A Levels. She looks about fourteen so I don't suppose anyone will object, and she certainly is not likely to play contact sports below her age-weight ratio, being light enough to pick up with one hand. Not that I tried.

Next came Hong Kong, where the speed of life suddenly shoots up a few gears and one finds oneself, ludicrously, trying to keep pace with the others by faxing with one hand, phoning with the other and interviewing with what's left, all at once. It's like a maelstrom, where everyone seems to need to be seen to be busy all the time. I cannot imagine anyone ever just slobbing about in front of the telly in Hong Kong. So when, in the middle of queues of interviews, Tim Fok, whose father Henry has since the war owned the concessions on all the sand brought into the colony, suggested we go over to see his new city at Nansha in China, it is a welcome respite. The 36-hole golf course in the middle of the city has apparently involved shifting more earth than the new airport at Lan Tau. The whole enterprise is conceived on a massive scale and includes the construction of a deep-water port at the mouth of the Pearl River. The idea is that Millfield may be asked to establish a satellite school in one of the valleys alongside this course, though I'll believe this when I see it. Tony, the competent Irish contractor, shows us around and at one point we come across a huge tree in the middle of the wilderness of mud, propped up by poles on all sides. I ask him what's special about it. 'What's special about that tree is that it wasn't there yesterday.' Such is the pace of change.

Next up, Beijing. For this leg, we were accompanied by Dr Simon Ly, a polyglot Cambodian, educated in the UK and the USA, and charged with looking after us by Mr Li Shou Goa, he whose family had been adopted by Deng Xhiaoping and whose son is now at Edgarley. As such, Mr Li enjoys special privileges among the Chinese elite. Thus not one but two new Audis meet us at the airport. The second, apparently, was for security, though from what or whom we were being made secure was never entirely clear.

The main purpose of this visit, however, is to meet William Louey, a young Old Millfieldian whose grandfather had founded the Hong Kong bus and tram company, and to interview those pupils whom he has identified as being the *crème de la crème* of the academic elite of Beijing's schools. Those who we agree will benefit from the whole Millfield experience will receive full funding from William both at school and at their University subsequently. The five we meet are astonishing. All are majoring in maths and physics, yet their English is fluent. At the end of each interview I ask, as always, if they have any questions.

'Yes, Mr Martin. Please, what were you doing last March 13?'

'I can't remember. What were *you* doing?'

'It was the eclipse. I went to the zoo with a thermometer to observe changes in the animals.'

[48]

'And were there any?'

'Sadly, no.'

After this, I am less surprised but equally stumped by the next question: 'Is it true that the Greenwich Observatory has been moved?' These are exceptional students by any standard. Indeed, these, our first cohort, all subsequently went on to read maths or science at either Oxford or Cambridge, having qualified in two cases for membership of the British Mathematics Olympiad in all but nationality.

Lunch with Ma Wen Suey, one of the twelve national Vice-Premiers. Tight security, a flurry of aides, guards and waitresses in pink livery. Suddenly, there he was, slap on time, with his wife and westernized daughter. He looked exactly like Mao, the same hair, the suit, the unlined face. He has an undeniable aura, and fortunately, an emergent sense of humour. I had earlier heard him referred to as Ma Lau, and during lunch innocently attributed this title to him. There was a shocked silence all round the table, and then he roared with laughter. It transpired that this means Old Man Ma. Experience is what you get five minutes after you need it! The expressions on his aides' faces at this gaffe will remain with me for ever. The family stayed for two hours over a lunch comprising vegetables, fish, meat, Beijing duck, rice, soup, sweets and fruit. As they left, they issued warm invitations to come and stay any time we found ourselves in their city again.

While this was at the Grand Hotel just by Tiananmen Square, supper that night is in a very modest little cafe. This time though, it is with the Director of Education for Beijing and two of his key players, responsible respectively for the city's 500 secondary schools and for all Further Education: the top brass. The discussion, with Simon as our translator, is centred on my ideas to foster teacher exchanges with the UK, ideas which they are kind enough to take seriously. Indeed they evince real enthusiasm and as we munch our scorpions, which they have thoughtfully ordered for us, I begin to think a successful scheme could be put together. Sadly, in the event all my subsequent letters remained unanswered and I had to assume eventually that other priorities had taken over. But it was fun breathing ozone at that level for a bit, even if there were no results to justify it.

A day off to visit the Great Wall. A carnival atmosphere, even on the steeper sections of this astounding phenomenon—and they are *very* steep. On the way back in our Audis, we turned off the main road onto dirt tracks to visit the collective farm where one of our drivers had worked for two years as a labourer during the Cultural Revolution. He had not been back there since. The heroic mural he had helped to paint still exhorted corporate effort from the side of the only two storey building in the village. We were invited by Mrs Zhou, our driver's former 'landlady', to have supper in her home. A whole meal seemed to occur from nowhere with bean curd, peanuts and beer. Humbling hospitality offered to complete strangers by people with very little food to spare.

After this, it was weird to be sucked back into the jet stream of international travel. We left Beijing at midday, flew to Heathrow via Paris and drove to Street where I was able to put in an appearance at a farewell dinner for three retiring colleagues, dropping into the conversation casually, 'When I was having lunch in Beijing this morning...'.

Chapter 4

A sculpture subsides under its own weight

MAY 1996. As I went round Shapwick House yesterday evening John in the Upper Sixth told me that he had just been accepted for a course in Mechanical Engineering and Japanese, perhaps the least predictable combination I have yet encountered. Talking later that evening with a group of third-formers, I thought I saw a girl slipping into one of the rooms arm in arm with a boy. My suspicions were immediately red hot and I had already begun to remonstrate with them before I realized that she was in fact his mother, making an unscheduled visit. My mistake was not, I think, entirely unwelcome to her and she promised not to keep her embarrassed son from his prep for too long. The event reminded me of the occasion early in our time here when, looking for a boys' dormitory, we had opened a door deep in the labyrinth of Kingweston House, to find it had a bath in it, and that this was occupied by a fifth-former. He seemed to take it in his stride. 'I'll be out in a moment, Sir.'

The Tutor for Admissions is told that a 'top Russian official' wishes to visit us with her son. This turns out to be Boris Yeltsin's daughter, Tatyana, and her son, also called Boris Yeltsin. Security is tight in prospect, but in practice turns out to comprise no more than a very capable friend of the family who also acts as translator. The boy is a good looking, rather distant chap, but a fine tennis player and obviously pretty bright, with excellent English. The security issues are going to grow however, and with a name like his, regardless of the family's wish for anonymity, it won't be long before the press are on to it, I'm sure.

Today we are hosts to ten prep school Heads who visit us for the afternoon and for dinner. All are full of praise for the helpfulness of our pupils and for the unusually friendly atmosphere in the school. Indeed, the pupils never seem to let us down with strangers on campus; I could not ask for more. In a discussion session with the Heads, I am asked what it is that generates such a feeling and on impulse, I suggest that rather than getting my views, we should sally forth to hear what the first people we encounter have to say on the matter. My heart does sink slightly when the first pupils we see coming round the corner are three of our less prepossessing fourth-form girls. Nevertheless, as the Heads cluster round, I put the question to them 'Where does the spirit in the school come from?' They are entirely unfazed either by the situation, the audience or the question and answer pretty much with one voice, 'From the people, Sir.' Moments like this reinforce my conviction that I have the best job in Britain.

A visit today from a boy just back from a six-month teaching commitment in Uganda with Students Partnership Worldwide which has had an immense impact on him, so much so that he is going to change his university course to Development Studies. He told me of an acquaintance in Jinja, who had got so plastered that he had staggered into the bush and fallen asleep. It seems that the poor chap had then been attacked by a lion 'which made off with most of his buttocks.'

It is 7.20 a.m. by the pool. A sleepy Edgarley boy is sitting on the ground outside, fully clothed, staring vacantly into space.

'Are you bored?' I ask inanely.

'No, Sir,' he replies locking his brain into gear, 'I'm a day boy.'

Today two cases appear that both illustrate the harm done to youngsters by rich, neglectful parents. The plight of the one youngster is drawn to my attention by his tutor, who is clearly very concerned for him. The chap is only thirteen, but he has not been allowed home for three years. Now he has had another letter from his mother telling him that he will spend next holiday at a summer camp in Europe. Again. One can only guess at what the long-term effects of such rejection can be. In the short term, despite his natural reserve, the boy is showing signs of real distress. I must clearly confront the parents with the situation they have created, and urge them to review their plans for their son.

In the second case, the boy desperately wants to be at home with his family, but they vigorously oppose the idea, arguing that he is spoilt at home by the servants and that he needs to confront the demands he faces here, rather than running away from them. Put like that, I sympathize with the parents, but the boy is so determined to go back to his mother that he has started stealing in order to force my hand. He tells us, however, that if he is sent home by me, his father will beat him and lock him up. It's a real dilemma. What would the Children Act advise? Eventually, after much correspondence, many faxes and umpteen phone calls, a relative is sent over to set up home locally so that the poor boy can both be 'at home' and finish his courses here at the same time. A compromise, of course, but the best we could work out.

At today's service in Wells Cathedral, the Dean tells of the Austrian psychiatrist looking at an Alp from his window. On one side a path threads laboriously to the summit, while on the other a cable car sweeps majestically to the same point. For those arriving from both sides, the view is the same, but the vision is entirely different: no gain without pain. It is a poignant example of what I keep on about to the school in my assemblies, but the Dean put it much better than I ever have.

A quad message from Giles Neeve surfaces in the in-tray: 'James has been variously troublesome and ungracious in maths, music and physics; smug and uncooperative. He tells me he has been brought up to believe he has the same right as anyone else to say what he pleases. I relieved him of this misapprehension. Head of Year gated for a week.'

A great relief to be able to interview Kevin Spears, the outstanding British Council Librarian whom I'd met in Delhi, for our librarian post. After the conventional and unimaginative people we'd seen last week, he was a breath of fresh air and I offered him the job on the spot. He is a maverick MBA in Management Studies, and having successfully computerized the Indian library, he sees the need to revolutionize ours. Then lunch in the dining hall with a group of sixth-formers and a prep school Head from Kent, with whom an instant rapport was struck. Apparently, he had thought of flying down in his two-seater plane but the weather decided him in favour of driving his twin-seater Porsche instead. He was very quick to recognize the prevailing atmosphere in the school, with which he identified instinctively.

Tea with four local councillors in sombre mood, contemplating the light pollution threatened by our plans for a double Astro Hockey complex. In other circumstances I would have sided with them over this, but I bend my instincts in favour of the school's long-term interests, as I must. Their visit recalled for me the occasion recently at the pre-prep school when the headmistress was awaiting an important visit from two town councillors to discuss a planning application. On arrival, they were intercepted by a 4-year-old girl who invited them immediately to have tea with her. Assuming that this was all part of the official Reception Committee, and clearly entranced by the warmth of the welcome, the councillors manfully accepted her invitation and soon found themselves bent double, squeezing into the Wendy House behind their diminutive hostess. Once they were all squashed in, she poured three imaginary cups of tea and struck up a conversation with them. Some minutes later they were all discovered in this cramped space by the Head, who had been alerted to the fact that the councillors were on site and had been frantically searching for them for some time.

Three representatives of Renong, one of Malaysia's top ten companies, come to see us. They want us to establish, staff and run a new sixth-form college near Kuala Lumpur at Proton City on a one hundred acre green field, or raw jungle site. It is to be a boarding school for 300 selected boys and girls. It will be a huge project if it gets off the ground, with endless possibilities for exchanging not just pupils between the two schools but also staff. What a mouth-watering prospect! They want to open in January 1998, so we must certainly get our skates on.

Last term it was Deng Xiaoping's adopted grandson. Last week, Yeltsin's grandson. Today, Brezhnev's grandson, together with two top Russian tennis players. Or are they minders, masquerading as pupils? It will be interesting to see who adapts to us most, and least, easily. Also two Indian families from our trip earlier in the year, and a visit from one of our Doon School exchange people who wants to stay on here to complete his A Levels. I feel these are real coups for Millfield and take new heart for the dying days of the term, when the absence of the A-Level year in the exam halls decapitates the school, removing any possibility of generating a fitting climax to the year.

There can't be many schools in which a £1 million consultancy in Malaysia and a new English as a Foreign Language Centre come up in a governors meeting under A.O.B.

'Toff schoolboys mark own exams.' I can see the headline writers having a field day. The news comes through from Edgarley that two of our tutors are reported to have passed the entrance exam scripts they should have marked to their fourth-year sets to mark in class. This is a damaging accusation of unprofessional action which must be followed up. The rest of the day goes by in a flurry of parental visits: Mrs Terai with her translator from

Tokyo about the pleasant but bone idle Fumi, one of the girls I'd seen in Hanoi; a family I'd met in Bombay; and finally a Spanish family from Washington. And it is also the day which marks the end of the trouble with the housemaster who lost his two house tutors in such quick succession. To lose one may be regarded as a misfortune, but to lose two...We have had to buy him out of his House for a large tax-free sum, just as the indiscipline over which he has carelessly presided comes to a head.

Three concertos in a single evening: Emily Crump played a Mozart flute concerto, Kate Rees played the Bruch violin concerto and Isabel Claisse the Dvorak cello concerto, all accompanied by our forty-piece orchestra, only six of whom are leaving this term.

The term is not over yet, though, and to remind me, three naughty girls are gated for drinking. Their respective parents' reactions to the news are instructive. One parent calls me to threaten legal action against the school for allowing her daughter to drink and for not examining the incontinent, foul-mouthed girl on admission to the medical centre. Another arrives late and unannounced at her daughter's House, terrifies her room-mates and others by screaming at her that she 'will be working in a factory at 9 tomorrow' before dragging the horrified girl away, only to ring the next day to say she will be returning her daughter at lunchtime. And the third calls me to apologize for his daughter and to thank us for taking action to impress the seriousness of her offence upon her. Three basically pleasant little girls who have all made the same mistake, generating a considered disciplinary response here, but eliciting three staggeringly different responses from their parents.

Two entirely new parental obsessions today. First, a mother demanded to see me personally without any warning, incandescent with fury, because her son, who had been suspended, had missed the leavers' photo and what was I going to do about it? Nothing short of gathering all 250 leavers together for a reshoot would satisfy her, she asserted through clenched teeth—a totally unrealistic prospect.

This was followed by a bitterly estranged couple fighting not about their poor daughter, but about her horse. Father says we must resist any move by his ex-wife to remove the horse. Mother, who is hell-bent on doing exactly that, takes an altogether more dramatic line and says the father 'has trained our daughter to beat me up, which she did last week.' I'm inclined to adopt a Solomon-like stance over this and offer two equine legs each—split the difference and be done.

Nick Bollettieri himself breezes in, just off a plane from Florida, and immediately falls in love with the school, which obviously endears him to me. He talks to a full theatre of enthusiastic youngsters about his philosophy of competitive sport, teaches various tennis clinics very engagingly and comes to dinner. Sadly, Brezhnev's daughter, visiting the school, leaves just as he arrives. I would have enjoyed introducing an elegant Russian grandee to this ageless, bronzed American narcissist. Just as he leaves the next day, a Thai princess arrives, so no luck there either in terms of multi-cultural engagement. The mother confuses me by looking exactly the same age as her graceful daughter. When I make the obvious mistake, she appears quite pleased, though her daughter's reaction was understandably different.

Every year we offer an open invitation to sculptors to compete for a commission. This involves creating a work on campus, which we are developing as a sculpture park. The construction itself takes place in the middle of the school during the summer term, so that all pupils can follow its development at every stage of the creative process. This year's winner of the annual sculpture commission is on tenterhooks as a JCB hoists his splendid structure into position outside the new swimming pool. The bottom half settles easily into place, but the top half, to our and particularly his horror, starts to buckle as it subsides from the upright position it was intended to hold.

'It's knackered like me,' sighs poor David in despair after ten weeks of ceaseless labour in his tented pavilion in the middle of the campus, 'I need a structural engineer.'

I am not surprised, given that the whole thing is twelve-feet high and weighs a ton and that we have been suggesting this to him for some time. At least the bottom half, which is now all that will be in place for Parents' Day, resembles a butterfly swimmer, which is apposite. Perhaps we should settle for that and sell the other half.

Parents' Day. A gale of wind but no rain, so the record for dry days for this event is sustained. This is such a long-standing record now that it has become part of local folk-lore. The days of the Head who presides over a wet Parents' Day will surely be numbered. We feed the 4,000 again, most of whom pitch up in the marquee for the prize giving and the end of year Service. After lunch, there is much sobbing and gnashing of teeth on the golf course as the leavers come to terms finally with the fact that they really are leaving not just the school but all their friends as well. It is a highly charged, emotional day for everyone. At six, when everyone has left, Julia and I go up to my room to pick up a couple of little gifts, sit down for a moment... and wake up an hour later.

During the last week of term kind parents have given me a little box from India, a bigger box from China, a CD of Schubert's Quintet in C, a small rose bush, and a brightly coloured plate in the shape of Sri Lanka. All these are much appreciated, the more so perhaps for the fact that I have done little to deserve any of them. Fortunately, there are no semi-cured leather handbags from Nigeria, of which one houseparent tells me he is reluctantly accumulating quite a collection. I wonder if I should declare these items as benefits in kind for tax purposes, but decide against it.

Sarah Champion, who has held the fort as acting Head at Edgarley with great flair this year, was interviewing a little boy from Australia last week. Eventually she asked him if he had any questions for her. He apparently thought for a moment and said, 'Yeah. D'yer know any jokes?'

Eleven days into the holiday and reports are finished with around 40,000 pieces of paper compiled, scrutinized, studied, analysed, sorted and clamped together by tutors and the secretarial staff. Among my favourites this term are: 'Despite his devotion to swimming, he is keeping his head above water', 'She has improved her feel for Harry' (happily, Harry turns out to be a horse), 'His gift for frivolity is never corroded by the work ethic', and, of a talented golfer, from her group tutor, 'She has par in most courses and a few birdies and eagles. Only in French is she stuck in a bunker.'

A three-hour meeting on the strategic plan with Paul Oddie, the Bursar, who has done this sort of thing for the Army, and David Rosser, the deputy head, considering departmental contributions. Understandably, most contributors are concerned with their own processes but a few have really put their Heads above the parapet to survey the wider school horizon. We conclude that there are seventeen ideas worth pursuing. There were also some engaging but less than practical ideas, among which were: the need for senior management to encourage tutors to write more books, down-sizing the school, ignoring the National Curriculum, and hiring a member of staff with sufficiently broad shoulders for the other tutors to cry on. Funnily enough, I have always thought that was my job.

I drove to Trent Bridge for the final of the Lord's Taverners cricket competition against Shrewsbury. The county really push out the boat for us to ensure that the boys have a day to remember. Mind you, they are unlikely to forget it, having survived countless earlier rounds spread over two seasons to make it this far. The vast score board is fully manned, just as it was three days earlier for the Test match against India, and even the member of staff who opens the gate on to the pitch for incoming batsmen was on duty for the occasion. Shrewsbury were 127 all out at lunch, and I, and I suspect other Millfield supporters, were suffused with a hopefully imperceptible glow of confidence that we were likely to prevail. At 30 for 2 off twenty overs, this had evaporated and at 80 for 6 we were looking down the barrel of defeat. Then Jasper Gilbey, 13 years old, and undaunted by our predicament, cheerfully completes an innings of 54 not out and wins the match for us. The stuff of heroes! We have now won this most prestigious competition something like eight times in the last twelve years—an amazing tribute not just to the boys but to the quality of the coaching they have received from their tutors. These are professional teachers, not sportsmen, who are of course hired primarily for their classroom skills and who undertake their cricket coaching out of love of the game and the fulfilment of seeing their team develop. In this case, the team would go to the ends of the earth for Mark Smith, their coach, who has a quite exceptional rapport with the boys.

Our arrival at our remote home in France for our holiday surprises the pine marten, with whom we have a sort of time share. He or she has clearly been busy using the kitchen for its designated purpose, for the floor is littered with bits of rabbit, birds, mice and even pheasant legs and breast bones. Only later, having cleared up, sitting on the grass outside, listening to the oriole, watching a deer grazing opposite, the black redstarts playing in the barn, a wren eating our mulberries above us and the bats beginning to zoom around the courtyard, do we feel that the school year is over and that the holiday can really begin.

A few days later I fly back to school to open the World Catholic Games, which we are hosting at Millfield this year. Over 1,000 athletes from thirteen countries are living in the school for a week and competing in a variety of different individual and team sports. We won the booking against hot competition from one British and two European universities, thanks to the tenacity and organizing ability of our Estates manager.

I speak in French, which is the Games' *lingua franca*, and then in English, as requested, presumably for the benefit of francophobes. At the champagne reception afterwards, a French delegate flatteringly asks me if, given my accent, I am from Lille. Unfortunately, she is from Lyons, so it's a less flattering question than I had at first hoped.

Chapter 5

Morality and Mortality are confused

AUGUST 1996. I return for my office to find my desk has disappeared under paper. It takes a couple of days before the bottom of the in-tray looms into sight. In the meantime, among a galaxy of varied pieces of correspondence, I have unearthed three complaints about the reports, ten requests for bursaries, and a couple of nasty ones, which get the bowels churning again. The first is from the parents of the day girl whom we referred last term to Social Services, following the discovery of inexplicable marks on her body. Our procedures in case of suspected abuse are endorsed by the local DSS office as being exemplary, and we followed them to the letter. Her parents provide no new views on why they think we mishandled the situation and clearly still feel very raw, which I can understand, and defensive, which I cannot. I had expected them to be glad that we had taken the signs of their daughter's injuries seriously. Not at all!

The second is a scandalous suggestion from a parent in Pakistan that his son suffered 'torture' at the hands of tutors and pupils last term, before being removed without consultation, owing a term's fees. The ease with which some parents who default on fees are able to dream up accusations of this kind to cover their tracks is breathtaking, but this one takes the biscuit.

By way of compensation, one parent has written to congratulate us on our 'swift and cheery' approach at the Service and the prize-giving back in July. 'My wife was less certain about the girl in the bathing costume who led the Lord's Prayer, though personally I thought it added rather an exotic touch.' I remember the dress and its owner well. Both were adventurous. The latter, with or without the former, later became one of David Cameron's A-list parliamentary candidates.

Yeltsin's grandson and namesake Boris starts this term with his resident bodyguard—resident, that is, in a hotel in Street. He is accompanied from Moscow by the son of Chubais, the chief of staff in the Kremlin. I expect we will have to conform to some fairly tight security arrangements, though none have been mentioned to date. We will call young Boris 'Eltsin', which may put people off the track long enough for him to establish himself here as just another sixth-former.

Fat chance! The national press has got hold of the story from a local reporter and is in full cry. Yeltsin now, Brezhnev next year and the name of the Russian Embassy press attaché happens to be Gorbachev. My birthday starts at 6.30 with the first call. Between then and lunch, there are fourteen interviews, including Izvestia, the *Moscow Times*, the BBC World Service, ITN News, and ZDF in Germany who promise, or rather threaten, to send a TV crew once term has started. There is mild concern in the Russian Embassy about all this, but no panic. Indeed, more anxiety is expressed by Zhang Li's parents and guardians about the fact that his connection with Deng Xhiaoping has somehow surfaced in all this. In the light of the frenzied interest taken in him now, it seems odd that he has been here for a year already without anyone outside the school having noticed.

A visiting Indian MP has seen the Yeltsin news in the *Times of India*, a tutor read about it in a local Austrian newspaper, *Il Messaggero* are sending a reporter hot-foot to cover the story and the World Service is going to do a feature on a day at Millfield.

Friends in America have seen a half page article on the school in the *New York Times* and my daughter's mother-in-law rings from New Zealand to say she has seen me on television. Such wide publicity cannot of course be bought at any price. Now all we have to do is to try to see that the poor chap at the centre of all this is given the space by the rest of us to get to grips with his new school like any other of the 350 new pupils we welcome this term.

The first day of term and a poor third-year boy who is homesick nevertheless has the presence of mind to find his way to the Bursar's office.

'I have been told that you look after the money here,' he says, 'Can I have some please to buy a ticket home?'

A colleague and his wife find me in the lunch queue and ask me if we could talk somewhere quietly. It is obviously serious and we go up to my room for a cup of tea.

They have just been told by their consultant that he has a tumour and that the bone marrow is also infected. He is forty-eight, in the prime of his life in every way, a good mathematician and an outstanding rugby coach. The long-term prospects are not good. What on earth can one say? It is a ghastly moment. His fortitude is humbling, and remains so throughout the coming six months. I dissuade him from actually running his rugby practice, which is what he was planning to do in half an hour.

A Saudi Head has written supporting a prospective pupil. 'He is of good fame, behaviour and morals.' Even so, I harden my heart, for the 'boy' in question sports a beard and turns out to be nineteen already.

I read somewhere last week an extraordinary piece of information. Apparently two hundred years ago the biggest prime number was 10 digits, one hundred years ago it was 20 digits, and now a computer has done its homework and has come up with a prime number that is 2 to the power of 1,257,787-1, which is over 300,000 digits long. I told my assemblies this morning that if this is any sort of index of the speed at which knowledge is expanding, they have my most profound sympathy.

The priority this first week has been to try to settle all our new entrants as painlessly for them as possible. Houseparents have run outings and competitions of all kinds in the evenings and on Sunday, and happily the sun has shone. This makes an immense difference to the whole feeling in the school. A wet first week can be really bad news. Even so, both our counsellors have had exhausting weeks and look pretty drained. With this in mind, I thought I had spotted a lost soul in the dining hall, from the Doon School as it turned out, and sidled up to him to see if he needed help.

'Oh no thank you, Sir. I have just had my lunch. Delicious, Sir. Curry. Just like at home. I had really quite a generous portion, Sir.'

At least I don't think we need worry about *him* for the moment.

Carl arrives to join the sixth-form. He is six foot eight and weighs twenty stone, which is just as well for he is the GB hope of a medal at shot putt in a couple of Olympics' time. We have to make a special bed for him. When he comes through my door, it's like a full eclipse of the sun. He proves to be a genial young man, with whom everybody of both sexes and all ages feels immediately at home. While it is clear to us all that Carl is here for our athletics facilities—and his three A Levels—it is less clear why this weekend the talent scout from Oklahoma pitches up to see our tennis players in action. I ask our resident Bollettieri coach why he has come.

'Because last year the Kansas scout spoke us up big time,' he says.

It is rather gratifying to know that we are on the big American university talent-spotting circuit.

Boris's bodyguard is Sergei. He is a pleasant young man who must be bored stiff all day, but who materializes in Boris's House in the evenings to play pool after prep. His English is poor, but he seems to have been accepted without question by the other boys, possibly because he claims to be able to kill a man with his bare hands. Apparently, indeed, they have presented him with a House tie.

At a houseparents' meeting during a discussion on eating disorders, I hear myself say, 'The tip of the iceberg has been unearthed.' I must be losing my grip on the English language.

The British Council Director in Moscow rings. He is due to do an interview later today on prime-time TV in Moscow on the Boris story. Together, we try to turn the emphasis in favour of the quality of British independent schools generally and of boarding schools in particular. This seems wise, especially as a number of inexplicable events has occurred around Boris's boarding house during the last few days, which suggest we should try to play down where possible our routines. First, two men, who were not BT engineers, were spotted up a nearby telegraph pole. Then the houseparent's phone is cut off, there is a buzzing in his sitting room, an unmarked helicopter hovers over the House and there are three anonymous e-mails all asking about the security arrangements. Special Branch will come tomorrow to check it all out. Or have we just been reading too much le Carré?

The parents of some of our ten polo players have been pressing for greater subsidies from the school than we already give. This strikes me as greedy so we do some research among the eight schools who competed at Windsor in the summer to see how our competitors treat their polo players. At the same time we take stock of all the costs to Millfield of putting up our teams. To my surprise, it looks like £3,000 a year each and the research shows our subsidy is far higher than that offered elsewhere. We will try to put it on a self-funding basis from now on. Greed gets its come-uppance.

A girl takes an overdose of twelve Anadin tablets. She is admitted to hospital and is taken home eventually by her mother, herself a child psychologist, amidst recriminations that we have not taken sufficient care of her. Her mother then arranges for her to see another psychologist at home, and this one manages to persuade mother that the girl's problems are home-based and not at school. To her credit, the mother becomes much more co-operative at this point, greatly easing our assiduous houseparents' role in their duty of care at school.

Yesterday the senior soccer squad took off for Manchester for the day. In the morning they watched Manchester United training and met the players, Giggs, Cantona et al. In the afternoon they played last year's school champions, St. Bede's, and won 3-2. No wonder our top scorer called it the best day of his life.

Today was the sort of day that seems to happen more often these days, when I seem to talk to people without a break, in this case from 7.30 until 2.20. Then two solid hours with the Executive Group to discuss the plans for the new pavilion at Kingweston and moving the new tennis coaching system into Edgarley. This was interrupted by the welcome news that we have won the competition to host the 1998 Junior World Chess Championships. Then a pause for a cheese and tomato sandwich.

Lindsay Staniforth, talking at a meeting of Heads of Department on English as a Foreign Language, quoted Evita from Slovenia who declared last year, 'When I first came, everything sounded like porridge. When I left, everything was much easier. Everything sounded like sausages.'

Allie is sent to see me: a charming, intelligent, girl and a fine athlete, with the smoothest sprinting action I have seen. She is suffering from a loss of self-esteem, which has incapacitated her, and now she has lost three kilos in ten days. She was already taken off games but had tried to sneak back into aerobics, and she has been failing to keep her appointments with the counsellor. I have to point out that accepting medical advice is a condition of staying here, but I think she will find every loop-hole we allow her rather than work to arrest this dreadful eating disorder to which she is now prey. It would be a tragedy to lose her.

This week, though, we *have* lost a boy for smoking cannabis. His father is a Norwegian lawyer with a face so bereft of expression that it makes the Easter Island carvings look like Tom and Jerry. He charges us with deserting his son and is apparently oblivious to the boy's part in his demise. If only I could tell him what the son has already told us about his home life.

Rob Decamp, as Director of Studies, has to field a variety of parental queries about the curriculum, but no father is more pressingly insistent than the Judge. Rob has developed a quietly effective knack of coping with him. At each point that he is interrupted on the phone, he remembers where he was in his own sentence, waits until the rant has ended, and then carries on exactly where he had left off as if nothing had happened. This achieves two admirable objectives: allowing Rob to convey the relevant factual information, and infuriating the Judge.

Kevin Spears, our new Librarian, has just been appointed OBE for services with the British Council to Indian library services. He is relishing the freedom of action he has here to think radically about the future of our library as a resource centre. I have told him that, when he reports, anything short of revolution will be disappointing. We have to change the whole culture as accepted by the pupils, from a sweat-shop for the sixth-form, working in silence, to a stimulating multimedia base for all pupils, especially the younger ones.

I deal with the problem of one boy who does not want to go home, with good reason, but whose parents are insisting that he should be put on a plane home to Saudi within two days. I will not allow him to be manhandled on to a plane, even if any carrier would agree to take him under such circumstances. So I try to persuade his mother to come and collect him. I am beginning to realize that a working knowledge of Saudi law would be an asset for any headmaster of Millfield, and must remember to add this to my successor's job description. The whole thing reminds me of Francesca, who, three years ago, summoned home by her father to Nigeria, ate her air ticket in the taxi on the way to Heathrow. This nonplussed our long-suffering driver, who then had no option but to bring her back to school. Two days later we tried again. The taxi stopped at a red traffic light within sight of the airport and Francesca, a gritty, feisty girl if ever there was one, did a runner. We will not go through all that again this time.

There is a vituperative letter from Mrs M. following my insistence that fees in lieu of notice will be charged, in the wake of her inexplicable withdrawal of her son without reference to any one here. She threatens legal action. Her son's housemaster, Peter Mills, a man of great experience and sagacity, not easily stirred to anger, writes to me at the end of an exasperated letter reporting on the withdrawal, 'If Lady Macbeth has sons, send them all to me, but please, no more sons from Mrs M.'

The House song competition stirs the cockles of my heart as always. The sight of nearly 1,000 singers, in away-match dress, singing the Slave chorus in Italian from memory is amazing enough, but for the Chinese, Vietnamese, Indian and Russian pupils, it's little short of miraculous.

Glasgow by air from Bristol for the Headmasters' Conference annual meeting. I asked the taxi driver if he was from Glasgow himself.

'No, I'm from Renfrew. We reckon as those Glaswegians still practise cannibalism.'

'But there's no evidence for that, surely?' I reply unimaginatively.

'No, perhaps not, but there's none to the contrary either.'

From the Physics department minutes of their weekly meeting: 'Partial eclipse of the sun. JDW has arranged this for 1.55 p.m. on Saturday. Help sought to open the dome.'

This week we have had two cases of 'Attention Deficit Hyperactivity Disorder.' High energy levels, impulsive behaviour and chronic difficulty in paying attention make these youngsters hard work for parents, teachers and indeed for those sharing dormitories with them. Initially some of us, myself included, I am ashamed to say, had difficulty in accepting that the condition is not wilfulness but a serious problem to be dealt with professionally. I am reminded of mononucleosis—the kissing disease—from which it was seen to be cool to suffer in the USA when I taught there in the 60s, especially if you were of high school age and male and if you regarded yourself as a stud. Only later did its medical basis become clear.

In the papers today we read that we are all suffering from information overload. Some commentators are tempted to conclude that we need a bunch of Taliban fighters who would do for us what they have just done for Afghan women—stop education altogether. The problem for western education increasingly, however, is the confusion between the need to develop young people in all aspects of their life, which is ultimately immeasurable, and the measurable provision of mere information. To confuse successful academic skills—the stuff of league tables—with the ability to lead productive and happy lives is to sell everyone short, for the one is clearly not leading to the other.

Exams in Morality are the government's most recent bright idea, with numerous politicians all staking out the moral high ground. So I did my assemblies this week on that theme. A colleague later asked a young boy what I had spoken about. Could he remember?

'Oh yes. It was all about mortality.'

That's taking a pretty long view of it all, I guess, but he was not altogether wrong, in that we are all destined to play our part in the carbon cycle at some stage.

Hugh Monro from Clifton and Tom Wheare from Bryanston came today for our termly unscripted lunch together. The main topic was the recent decision to deny teachers the right to take early retirement 'for the better working of the school', from April next year. This will have immense implications for every common room in the country.

Suddenly, apropos of nothing at all, Hugh said, 'Chris, I had a dream about you last night. You went up to collect an award from Prince Charles and he gave you a Hoover.'

What on earth would Freud say about that? It must be something to do with my nose. We remain good friends, nevertheless.

Tatyana Yeltsin comes to see me with Vladimir, her translator. She is a delightful, relaxed woman who laughs easily and is gracious in forgiving my only partly remembered Russian. She has familiar, maternal questions about Boris and is keen for him to be treated in exactly the same way as every one else, thankfully. The very next day, a three page article on her appears in the *Express* under the banner headline 'Tanya Yeltsin sets up new dynasty to rival Kennedy's'. The portrait painted of her in the paper bears no resemblance to the woman I met the day before.

The agenda for our cabinet meeting today included eating arrangements for girls with eating disorders, the counsellor's workload last week, which includes four homesick souls, two pupils reporting parental abuse, one holiday rape victim, one boy suffering from depression and five new cases of bulimia. We discussed the realisation that all signs across the campus point to 'Reception', while Reception is labelled 'Administration Centre'. We have the opportunity to host the World Junior Chess Championships, and the inter-varsity Modern Pentathlon, with the World Modern Pentathlon Championships looking at us for 1998. The scope of our discussions doesn't seem to diminish with time. I recall a primary school Head in Bristol pointing out his deputy at the end of a corridor.

'He thinks he's had forty years' experience but he's really just had one year's experience forty times.'

No risk of that happening here, it seems.

Fears are expressed by a senior tutor that there is a pocket of racial tension in his year group. A Hong Kong boy has offered a friend £60 to beat up two Japanese boys, both of whom are built like barn doors. The matter is investigated. Have there been racial gibes, insulting behaviour, ancestor abuse? Not at all! *Cherchez la femme.*

The boy who had issued the contract explained though gritted teeth, 'When F. took my girlfriend (who left last year) I had no option but to offer money like that.'

A sad day for the romantic heroes of his ancestors, but a problem which turns out to be easily defused.

I had lunch with two new Lower Sixth girls. One of them, who had started life here in September projecting an image of the ultimate ice maiden, now shows signs of thawing and indeed of genuine enthusiasm for life.

'It's friendly here,' she says, 'but also adventurous. You have to be brave and launch out.'

That's very astute, and I'm impressed, the more so when she adds, 'How do you stay sane, Sir?'

It's flattering to think that she assumes I am.

Edward Norman is driven down from York by my friend Richard Shephard to give a Friday lecture. He is dry, deep and closely argued, as you might expect of any Reith lecturer. But he is also devoid of passion and makes no concession at all to the age or internationalism of his audience. There is no inflection of the voice, no joke, no anecdote to enliven the hour, not even a twitch of the eyebrow to signify personal involvement in what he is saying. As always, I am wracked with anxiety about how it is all going down with the pupils. I feel my stomach churning. I need not have worried. It is an intellectual *tour de force*, and as he denies the existence of Family Values—families being, in his view, merely conduits for wider value systems—he provokes among the 500 sixth-formers a more heated reaction than we have enjoyed for some time. I am grateful to him and proud of them and recognize their involvement as being a great tribute to him. He stays the night and I discover in him a *Sun* reader, a *Daily Telegraph* columnist, ('I have never read that paper'), a claret drinker and weightlifter. And Faust: 'I am bored by it all.'

Saturday morning. The Ridings School has just blown up. Sixty pupils are said to be on the point of expulsion. The Head resigns and a state of educational emergency is declared. A tragic spectacle. That evening, Peter Mills, on duty, visits five senior girls, out for a drink, legitimately, in their assigned pub. They greet him with glee and spend twenty minutes in animated conversation together. As he leaves, a local drinker hovers up to him and says admiringly, 'I see you're not from the Ridings then.'

The Head of Games and Head of Golf come round at 8.30 a.m., visibly shaken by a recent loss against Milton Abbey whom they claim we would normally expect to beat with our second team. What's to be done? It adds significance to a visit yesterday to the Leadbetter Golf Academy in Kent by three of our senior staff, to explore the possibility of translating their operation to our own campus. Indeed, we could probably set it up here in time for September and will now plan to do so. I must not allow my legendary antipathy to the game to affect my commitment to the scheme.

Later in the morning, Special Branch officers are round to discuss security arrangements for our Russians. These now include code-words for use in a hostage situation. I am assured that there is no word of any such plot from their intelligence sources, and yet the escalation of security awareness does seem a little sinister, especially given the very relaxed approach evinced so far.

Good news, for him if not for us. Ian Power has been appointed Headmaster of Lord Wandsworth College, where he will flourish. He was almost the first appointment I made here, as Head of Physics, while still in his twenties, and the fact that he has also run both a boys' and a girls' boarding house equally successfully since then makes him well qualified for this post. He is teaching the four Beijing boys, who have just come one to four in Millfield's entry for the National Mathematics contest, ahead of all our home-grown Oxford and Cambridge maths candidates. Special problems are posed by the fact that Mandarin has no conditional tense, yet as a physicist he is constantly having to ask them, 'What if...?' They in turn find this speculative, platonic approach hard to come to terms with. How is it that the Beijing scholars are so much better mathematicians than even the best of our home grown pupils, who themselves will contend strongly for places at Oxbridge to read maths? No one really knows, but perhaps the Head of Maths comes closest to a solution when she says, 'Where British pupils do half a dozen examples of a problem, our Chinese pupils do twenty.' Yet somehow mere repetition does not really offer a totally convincing answer to the enigma.

Never leave a school in the ante-penultimate week of term. I drove up to London with Dennis Silk for the Thanksgiving dinner given by the Morehead Foundation for the UK selectors, of whom I am one, and selected scholars. Travelling back the next day, I read in the paper that Chubais is under investigation by the Public Prosecutor in Moscow, and arrive to find he is booked in to see me tomorrow. Is this to discuss his son's future with us if the investigation finds against him? Then the phone rings to say that our visiting speaker for this afternoon is called unexpectedly to Paris, the Head of Music at Edgarley is reported as having purloined a clarinet, our US exchange teacher is trying to leave mid-year having caused mayhem in the Maths Department, and a parent has accused a female member of staff of having a lesbian relationship with her daughter. Meanwhile, the boys and girls have been behaving perfectly.

A third-year girl was overheard being very upbeat about her French exam result.

'I got 33%.' Then after a moment of doubt, 'But I think it's out of a hundred.'

Rob Decamp, at a Heads of Department meeting, warns us that we are 'entering the penumbra of a grey area.' I know how he feels. David Rosser is fatalistic, 'It's been like that since time immoral.'

Three Sisters, with Abi Griffiths, Charlotte Whittaker and Sam Thorburn in the title roles. I only realized afterwards that, for the first time in a school production, I had been unaware throughout the performance of the casting, the set or even the actors' virtues, such was the power with which the play was performed.

The next night, it's the Christmas Ball. There are 300 people, DJs and little black dresses, a deafening eighteen-piece band. Casualties? One boy is sent home drunk. A girl totters for a moment, and we realize it's because her knee brace was only taken off that morning. Another sobs; she has swollen glands and had reported sick earlier. There is just one chap who is kept in the medical centre for observation overnight, a delightful Chinese boy with an impeccable record, for whom two drinks were just one too many.

It has been an emotional day. In the morning I was in Bristol for the funeral of one of the most original and enterprising boys I've known. Toby Thomas was at Bristol Cathedral School, but was killed on his bike as a medical student in London last week. Over 500 people crammed into the church to hear tributes to him, and to enjoy vivid, gleeful memories of this eccentric chap. Only Toby could attend the final assembly of his school career dressed in full armour, play the ukulele and the nose whistle and get AAB at A Level with a reading age that suggested that this was impossible. His smile, his willingness to help others and his complete absence of any urge towards street cred were his hallmarks. His parents invite the lorry driver, who ran into him and who is on the rack, to join them for the service, which he does. An inspired move.

Then that evening we went to Georgian Cottage, the boys' sixth-form House, for their Christmas supper, which this year had added piquancy, for they were saying goodbye to Mike Gilfillan, their twenty-three stone house tutor. In the middle of various tributes to him, Johnny Zhao stood up and announced that he wanted to sing his tribute in Mandarin. Johnny had heard yesterday that he had come top equal in the UK National Mathematics

Challenge out of some 26,000 entrants. The boisterous boys fell silent and he sang a hauntingly beautiful song in an entirely unfamiliar medium, received at the end with rapturous applause by everyone. He was quietly confident, and since he was clearly not trying for any gratuitous effect, he had a profound effect on us all. It was an unusual moment, and a very moving one, as much for the boys' response as for Johnny's accomplishment. There followed greetings to Mike in all the languages represented in the House: Spanish, Italian, Arabic, Turkish, French, Hindi, Mandarin, Japanese and German. Carl Myerscough, just voted Young Athlete of the Year, greeted him in Geordie.

I have had to expel Hannah for smoking cannabis. Her father lives in Cairo. Her mother, who runs a tented foot safari camp in the Matthews Range in Kenya, flies in to plead her daughter's cause. She is a striking woman in a bush hat, with dust still on her boots from the Land Rover journey to Nairobi. We plan how Natasha can study for her A Levels in a tent 200 miles from any urban centre, and conclude that, with help from us, she can. It is an extraordinary encounter—a touch of Ryder Haggard in suburban Somerset. Both Hannah and her mother subsequently write the most amazingly appreciative letters, which I re-read from time to time when my spirits start to flag.

At the end of term, I am embarrassed by the gifts brought to me by some of the pupils from Beijing and Hanoi. I know they cannot afford them, but they give them all the same, and I cannot refuse them. Helen Zhang gives me a lovely letter and a fan, Cuong a stitched flower picture and Arul, from Malaysia, a cricket tour T-shirt. They take the trouble to search me out to hand them to me.

Mike Gilfillan and I do two duets as he leaves, at the staff party and at the houseparents' dinner. The staff party is a cathartic annual ritual, and is a good measure of the school's maturity. We all quail at the thought that we may this year be the target of Norman Warne's or Dick Ransley's satire, and we are right to be wary. But no blood is spilt. Neither of them turn knives in wounds and the invisible line between teasing and hurting is respected. The new staff, all fifteen of them, sing in tune—they must have practised—and people let their hair down round the piano for hours afterwards as a pall of silence settles over the campus outside with the departure of our charges for their holidays.

Reports produce quite a rich harvest of memorable comments this time round: 'He needs to keep his centre of gravity lower', 'He should abandon the pretence that life is a conspiracy to bring about his downfall', 'Frankness is such a wholesome attribute but she seems to avoid it like the plague', and 'I am Sisyphus and Camilla is my boulder'.

There was an interesting climbing report, 'Leila climbed up until half-term.' And then there's Dick Champion's favourite from technology, 'He took all term to produce a good stool.'

Chapter 6

Millfield is compared to bad vodka

JANUARY 1997. It's a bitterly raw start to the next term and even the coolest pupils are bundled up warmly against the cold. One Bruneian boy comes to see me in a mild state of shock. He's experiencing for the first time temperatures which are about thirty degrees below what he's used to. I quickly close the window in my room and ask him what he's wearing. He has managed to squeeze himself into a coat, a jacket, two sweaters, two shirts, a T-shirt and, underneath everything, the pyjamas he could not bring himself to take off that morning. And underneath that, a vest.

But it is less amusing later that day to encounter Vanessa, a sixth-former, looking haggard and wearing just a shirt. It is this which prompts me to stop and talk to her as we pass in the middle of the campus. It turns out that her poor mother is now bed-ridden and is finding it hard to see. Throughout the Christmas holiday, Vanessa has been her carer, looking after all her needs, bedpans and all. She is also looking after two younger sisters and, in between times, is working for her A Levels. To cap it all, last night she alone of all the family was at her grandmother's bedside as she died, after which she needed to try to support and encourage her mother in her loss. This is a family which is on the At Risk register, with a violent, threatening father. It is obvious that she needs massive additional support from us and fortunately her housemistress and group tutor are just the people to offer it. For her own reasons, however, she declines offers of more formal help, and Social Services cannot overrule her. The burdens that some of these young people carry are truly humbling.

The first Executive Group meeting of the term is the moment when we have to prioritize for the governors' approval the various capital projects which are currently in our sights for completion over the next five years. The list is astonishing: two new Astro hockey pitches (£900k); a new classroom block at Edgarley (£750k); a new boarding house at Millfield (£850k); two new Edgarley boarding houses (£600k); a new dining hall (£3m); and a pavilion at the Kingweston fields (£200k). There is even reference to a friend of the school, and current parent, who has suggested that he might want to fund a sports complex at Edgarley and an indoor athletics track here, with seating for 2,000 spectators. If this were to come off, it would be the premier such facility in the country. It is a programme of daunting complexity, but our jaws drop more at the sheer nerve of the discussion than at its scale.

After washing up after Sunday chapel, Julia, Dick Boustead and I headed for the dining hall for lunch. Our short cut through the side door was locked, so we broke the rules and went, improperly, through the south entrance. The duty Prefect was Johnny Zhao, one of our Beijing scholars, and our illegal entrance did not escape his eagle-eyed attention. He accosted us and reprimanded us politely.

'Please do not do this again, Sir,' he said without a flicker of irony.

I promised him we would not and he allowed us to proceed. All in a good spirit, and with right on his side throughout. But there may not be another prefect in the school who could have carried that off.

The Times publishes an article saying, among other inaccurate and damaging things, that 'Boris Yeltsin calls his girlfriend on his mobile phone from class.' Inaccurate, because he does not, and damaging, because the impression is given that our tutors have no control of pupils even in their core academic activity. I challenge this with the editor, risking the charge that 'the lady doth protest too much.' Academics, and especially pompous headmasters, can't take a joke etc. Two weeks later I get a reply from a deputy managing editor, a two-liner: 'We note that you do not contest the main substance of the article, namely that you have banned mobile phones.' It's the sort of brush off I might have expected from a tabloid. How *The Times* they are a-changin'.

Stephanie, who is a long-standing employee and who cleans my room at school, often looks in if I'm working late. She is invariably cheerful and I enjoy her company. Tonight she tells me she is shocked because her father has just contacted her, for the first time after forty-five years. Does he live in Australia?

'No, this side of Bridgwater.'

Will she see him now? 'I think so. It must be nice to have a father.'

I bump into Will during a visit to his House. He's in the GCSE year and finding academic life tough at the moment. I try to encourage him and tell him that I failed the eleven-plus exam and yet seemed to find things making more sense to me later on. I don't know what to make of the fact that he didn't seem at all surprised by this news.

The advertisement for my job appeared in the press today and created a very funny feeling in me. The first phone enquiry came at 7.30 a.m. from the Head of a school in Northern Ireland. I'm not looking forward to relinquishing my role here. Where else could you get this much excitement? By lunchtime, Gary Hunt, our visiting lecturer, who had come to talk about climate change, had suggested gently that I might work with him at the Scientific Exploration Society. Networking seems to have begun by osmosis already.

Norman Warne, an inexhaustible and resolute Head of Year, is shown a film by the local branch of Tesco's. It looks as if two of our fifth-form boys are giving money to the ubiquitous passer-by to buy drink for them illegally. He borrows the film, brings it back to school and asks Tony in the media centre to freeze-frame it at the appropriate spots. He then circulates the blown-up frames among tutors, who recognize the boys in a flash. Norman, an old hand, then interviews them.

'I know you haven't drunk it yet [which he did *not* know]. Go and get it.'

'Oh, yes Sir, right away.'

And they did. This is the man who managed to trace President Moi's grand daughter, who had run away from her father as much as from school, even before Interpol could do so. It was he who suggested tapping her sister's phone, and when the contact call was made, it was he who then drove down overnight to a B & B in Brighton to rescue the poor girl and bring her back. With people like this around, it is maddening to hear, from time to time, business people talking about the need for teachers to square up to the 'real world.'

An intruder is reported at night at Overleigh, one of the senior girls' Houses, which stands in its own grounds on the edge of Street. A face is seen at a first floor window and not surprisingly the girls are all of a flutter. I go round to try to reassure them that all necessary measures will be taken to render them safe. The next day Jim Tancock, our maintenance guru, is round soon after dawn to assess the best sites for cameras and PIR lights, only to find that the latter have already been installed but the bulbs have blown, and their absence has not been recorded. On the principle of bees and honey pots, it's perhaps surprising that there are not more such incidents at Overleigh. All that we have to do now is to illuminate the honey pot and pray in the evenings for rain, the policeman's friend.

The photos for our Far East tour are taken at lunch today. They will be circulated later to the press in the countries I am to visit, and judging by past experience many will be published. Pupils from each country are asked to report outside Millfield House at specific times. Hong Kong, India, Indonesia, Singapore—they all pass off well enough. Then the Chinese youngsters arrive, and there is an immediate shift upwards in the level of animation. They actually crack jokes in English, having only arrived in September. Finally the seven Bruneians line up, corralled by the indomitable and diminutive Asmi, and pose with me somewhere around my midriff. As we leave to warm up inside, I ask them if they have had lunch. Luckily they all laugh, although they could have been forgiven for going for my jugular. It's Ramadan.

The Great Debate this week is 'When is Chinese New Year?' Many enterprising pupils are suggesting quite a variety of dates, all of which, to nobody's surprise, tend to suggest that the half-term holiday should be protracted to embrace it. Eventually we call the Chinese Embassy. Even they do not know. So we adopt a typical English compromise and declare that the Millfield Chinese New Year will be half-way between the extremes already suggested. Amazingly, pupils seem happy to accept this.

John, the most mild-mannered and courteous of boys, has celebrated his eighteenth birthday by drinking a bottle of German hootch brought from home, all by himself. Unfortunately this led to his running amok in his House and causing a good deal of minor damage. He is utterly mortified, as are we on his behalf, and has now retreated into himself again. He is normally the most supportive of people, though some of his suggestions on the School Council have indicated a political stance way off to the right somewhere. For instance, when we were considering ways of dissuading smokers from using the loos to practise their illegal habit, he suggested we fix paint sprays in all the cubicles, activated by smoke, so that the culprits could be identified subsequently.

I noticed hoof marks in the Jubilee pitch on my way in this morning and gather that a horse with a high equine IQ has learnt how to lift the catch of its stall and has spent the night grazing the headmaster's lawn. Fortunately it had no wider ambitions and thus was not tempted to take to the road with all the nightmare possibilities that might then have ensued. Needless to say, the stable manager is designing a new horse-proof lock.

Julia and I were going round a girls' House yesterday and met among others, Jane, whose twin sister is—at their joint request—in another House altogether. At home they share a room and are good friends, though Jane confides that 'I've only once hugged her in my life. I hate being mistaken for her.' This is the first time they have been formally separated and they are apparently coming to terms with their complex relationship for the first time here.

Today we opened the new indoor, three-court tennis centre, the biggest covered space in the school. There is an office, changing room, loos, weights room, balcony seating for several hundred people—the works. It was a low key affair just before lunch and I then went in to the dining hall to eat. I found myself sitting next to a couple of third-form boys who asked me what I'd been doing so far today. I told them of the tennis centre.

'Oh really Sir,' said one. 'Where is it?'

It was twenty yards away—we could see it plainly from where we sat—but they'd apparently never thought to enquire what all the works going on around them since they joined the school five months ago could possibly portend. I suppose at that age whatever you encounter is just normal, and you therefore accept it uncritically as a given in your new life. This must be one of the reasons for their resilience and adaptability.

Jean Hall, the consultant we have asked to construct, distribute and analyse a parental questionnaire, came to give us feedback on the results of her labours. It seems we have had a good response, with 85% of respondents confirming that they have had value for money. Girls' dress, my self-confessed Waterloo, is apparently the source of most concern. I just cannot get interested in it. It's not an excuse—I'm paid to be interested in it and indeed to get it right, I know—but other things seem to distract my attention every time I determine to do something. The truth is I feel that Millfield and uniforms are inimical, so any dress code is going to comprise mere guide lines. Teenage girls, as every parent knows, are adept at turning an innocent school shirt into something that even Mata Hari at her most seductive would have considered over the top, so guidelines are always going to present them with a creative challenge. Nevertheless, having seen schools where the poor girls are all cloned in kilts or brown sweaters, I prefer the variety we enjoy here and I guess the hassle of arresting those who go too far is worth it.

This has been a really bad week. The Deputy Headmaster is in Florida checking out the Bollettieri Tennis Academy. Sue Woods, who is in charge of girls, is on a teacher tour of South Africa. So it is this week that two senior pupils who both have impeccable records, a boy and a girl, spread the word that they have had sex on campus. Indeed there are those who tell staff that they have observed the event. The two people, with characteristic honesty, confirm this, and with the utmost regret I require them to leave. No co-educational boarding school Head could do otherwise. We are the biggest such school in the country, and the implications of *not* taking the hardest line are unimaginable. A hateful situation. Their families are distraught. Their friends are angry. Other parents, including a governor, come to see me with special pleading: such excellent kids—show mercy. Siren voices. Couldn't I turn a Nelsonian eye? The parents of both, one of whom is a single mother, see me more than once, naturally unwilling and actually unable to accept the situation. It is right that they fight for their children, but it as if they cannot see that no must mean no in this circumstance. I explain my position carefully to the staff and to the senior years, saying why I think I have no option but to do what I have done, but knowing the two young people pretty well and liking them a lot, I hate it. In a co-ed school there are certain things you just cannot do with impunity. I remember a friend with whom I had taught at Phillips Exeter in the States, who came to see me a year ago, having moved as Dean of Students to a different and very prestigious school on the East Coast. It had recently gone co-ed, and I asked him innocently what the main difference now was. I had not expected his reply: 'Pregnancies.'

In the middle of this, I have yet another broadside from the Judge. I take two hours, with a lot of help from various colleagues to reply to it. He relies on falsehood and innuendo. You can pin down the former and tackle the latter, with his son's help, but the tenacious Judge has a private agenda which I suspect is 'failure to educate a child to his full potential'—the ultimate unproveable charge. Knowing what his nickname is on the circuit helps assuage some of the pain he causes, but he has got under my skin and I resent it immensely.

'Alle guten Dinge sind drei,' and lo and behold in the same week comes poor Chris Gibson. It is confirmed that he has open TB. His mother flies over from the States. It's a huge public health issue. I write to all parents of people in his year, all 265 of them. There's a press release. A helpline is set up. The hospital in Taunton lines up X-rays for them all. The Somerset Health Authority has never known a case with so many possible contacts nor with such massive cost or logistical implications. We consider hiring in a mobile X-ray clinic to do it all on site but there are only a couple in the country and neither is available. There is widespread parental alarm, which the medical authorities and I do our utmost to allay. Chris himself seems fine. Indeed in a few weeks he is back at school, right as rain. Only a couple of contemporaries need second X-rays before being cleared. I am most concerned for Chris's room-mate, who lives in Burma, with a Burmese father and an Irish mother, but thankfully he too is given an all-clear.

There is a moment's light relief from these preoccupations at the HMC South West meeting. One colleague, who is in bitter dispute with his governors, points out how he has tried to introduce a 'lap-top for all' policy. It seems to have foundered eventually on chapel! They could not figure out where to store the machines in such large numbers when the pupils trooped into chapel every morning, leaving their academic hardware in piles outside. Is this another example of the church acting as a barrier to progress, albeit innocently in this case? No wonder the Reformation was so tricky.

A Hong Kong parent is moving to Somerset so that his son can enter the school as a day boy. He writes to ask if we would be willing to enter him officially on our records as a boarder, however, because then he would be eligible for a Hong Kong government grant. As a day boy, he would not be eligible. We look up the father's profession on the application form: Hong Kong Fraud Squad.

At the end of this really ghastly week comes a letter from Arul Suppiah's delightful mother in Malaysia, which certainly helps to soothe my troubled mind.

Dearest Mr Martin,

My hubby and I send our very good greetings. But the worst part is you leaving Millfield in 98 Summer. I am sure so many parents like me will miss you. Frankly speaking, I haven't met any Principal as lovely as you in many ways.

Surely she will go straight to Heaven. Her son is going to make a big name for himself as a cricketer. He is already an international player, having represented Malaysia at senior level. Two years ago he was thought to be the best bowler to go through the MCC coaching courses at Lord's, and came with a glowing reference from Sir Donald Bradman, which he proudly showed me on arrival.

The week of half-term was spent recruiting in Delhi and Bombay, staying with Vinu Baig and Cyrus and Katayun Engineer respectively. Katayun is the only former model I know to have fallen off a catwalk in Moscow into the lap of President Kruschev. A picture of this unlikely event was published on the front page of the *Times of India*, to Cyrus' bemusement. In Bombay, among the fifty or so people who came to the Millfield reunion was Sheila Pasricha, whom David Bailey had photographed as the woman who best represented Indian elegance. From such exotic company, I am brought down to earth by Ajit Singh's engaging but shy parrot. He lives on the terrace overlooking the sea, in possibly the most alluring setting enjoyed by any parrot anywhere. Whenever I approach him for a chat, he slowly but determinedly tips over until he has swung through 180 degrees and is hanging upside down. He has much in common with Marlene Dietrich, for no clearer indication of the wish to be alone could be offered.

I went up to Dehradun on the Shatabdi Express again to see the Doon School, where we set up an exchange last year, and to establish a similar one with its sister school for girls, Welhams. The headmistress, the tall and strikingly energetic Shanti Varma, was prodigal with her time, giving me a personal tour of her school at high speed, striding around the buildings, with me in hot pursuit. She clearly knows all her girls intimately. Her son-in-law is the novelist Vikram Seth, who is fortunate to have such an engaging mother-in-law.

The press coverage of my trip was extensive but totally misleading. The *Asian Age* carried an article which was guilty only of exaggeration, but the zenith of journalistic licence was achieved by the Bombay *Afternoon Despatch and Courier*. Under a big photo, they informed their immense readership that 'the whole Bruneian Cabinet send their children to Millfield' and that 'the school has 1,200 children, mainly the children of royalty or the captains of industry who are in any case the new royalty.'

I am back in Somerset, still jet-lagged, and balanced on a step ladder to try to reach the top of the in-tray, when in comes Tanya Yeltsin, husband Alexei, and Vladimir, their translator. There is much goodwill and laughter and I soon realize that they have come to reassure me that it is their intention that Boris will stay here, despite rumours to the contrary that have circulated in the press in Russia, in Germany, in India and here.

'We decide what Boris will do, not him.' And they leave on that forthright note to drive back to London again.

Mrs Kitiparaporn makes yet another visit from Thailand to discuss her pleasant but unambitious son. She cuts an exotic figure, impeccably dressed and manicured. This time she is accompanied by a Buddhist monk in saffron robes and shaven head, who turns out to be her husband, whom I have never met before. Where she is shrill and insistent, he is silent and genial, smiling an inner smile which hints at a relaxed attitude to the exigencies of everyday life. She tells me repeatedly that their son must go to Harvard—even though he has never been known to break academic sweat, and against all the evidence we have consistently presented. At one point she turns to her husband for support. There is a long pause, then, 'I like very much the view from your window.' That seems, in some magical way, to settle the matter and they leave, to my surprise, apparently pleased with the outcome of our discussion.

Two colourful notes on pupil misdoings arrive on my desk. 'Caroline, when apprehended in an amorous embrace with her boyfriend, offered in somewhat dubious mitigation that he was a good sportsman. She promised that it would not occur again.' There is in reality no such thing as a six-inch rule to be respected between pupils of opposite sex, but they all believe there is and I am certainly not going to disabuse them.

And the second. 'Camilla, whilst rollerblading to the video shop, lit up a cigarette, thus proving—unlike President Ford— that she could do two things at the same time. School gated and letter home.'

It is so refreshing to know that one's colleagues—most of them, anyway—still enjoy and are amused by the activities of the young, even when they are breaking the rules. It's not so hard to love the sinner while disapproving of the sin.

[87]

The new curricular programme, known as Dearing Mark Three after its inventor, is shaping up. We discuss it at length in the Heads of Department meeting. Breadth, AS and AL all enshrined in a National Diploma. All radical stuff. Unless of course you are old enough to remember the Highers of yesteryear.

Schadenfreude is a sin, I know, but I do get a special *frisson* of pleasure at the news that we have defeated Winchester College in *The Times* Chess Championships by five and a half games to a half. Our England Under 12 captain beat their England Under 14 captain. This will utterly confuse the press, who, whatever the evidence to the contrary, still like to think of us as a school for fast girls and slow boys.

At just the point at which I reluctantly decide I must do something serious about girls' dress, I get a call from the Deputy Head at Cheltenham Ladies College to enquire about the secret of our success in exactly this field. 'I gather your girls look really smart.'

Dino Tatanaki, who is known for his instinct for using the whole world as his wardrobe, left his bed in apple-pie order this morning, to the point where his housemaster, Dick Boustead, was going to commend him. This proved difficult, however, for it transpired that Dino had booked an illicit taxi that morning for Heathrow and was in Cairo by late afternoon.

Simon, our chaplain, is taken to hospital as an emergency admission. I have to rejig the Confirmation service, welcome the Bishop, talk to sixty All-Rounder parents, welcome a visiting lecturer, interview four geography teachers, conduct a two-hour senior houseparents' meeting, talk to the staff on the Soap Box, discuss swimming with the chief coach, talk to the confirmands and, as a very pleasant end to the day attend this year's dance extravaganza 'Expressive Edge' in the theatre. Still, it leaves no room for boredom.

The news from the hospital is cheering. Simon is on the phone and sounds pretty perky. Reading between the lines, which is not too hard with Simon, the nurses are clearly enthralled by him, and naturally he rises to the occasion as he does with any responsive audience.

'I'm between the sheets with Joanna Trollope,' he says archly, 'You should try it sometime.'

What was the diagnosis? 'Inflammation of the blood. I think.'

What? 'Oh blast, well perhaps not. I really should listen more carefully.'

He has had numerous blood tests. I am intrigued to know if they reveal more Bordeaux or Burgundy.

In the week in which the National Theatre Company runs workshops here on *Twelfth Night* with over 100 of our people, we hear that the Comédie Française want to include us on a tour it is organizing next term. It seems that word of our fabulous theatre has reached them in Paris, goodness knows how, and the clinching factor in their decision has been our tradition of performing annual French plays.

I call a meeting of the House charity representatives to discuss launching a new school-based charity effort. I explain the hard work which will inevitably be involved and try not to be too up-beat about it all, on the assumption that it is better to attract the strong for such a venture rather than rely too early on the fainter of heart. I ask those who, on reflection, are interested and can spare the time to come back to a second meeting next week, thinking that perhaps a third of the original thirty would do so. To my delight, all thirty show up. We're in business again, and to my immense relief, Lindsay Staniforth is willing to hold an umbrella over it all to ensure that good intentions are indeed translated into action.

Mike has always given everyone the impression that he doesn't have a care in the world, and is immensely popular as a result. Luck was on his side again recently when he was picked for the Welsh Water Polo team, even though, as he tells me, there is not a drop of Welsh blood in him.

'But I did once *know* a Welshman, Sir,' he assures me, by way of justification for his selection.

The quotes for the proposed new hockey pitches look pretty high and Astroturf, with a bid of £1.2 million, no longer look like our front runners for this contract. When we make this clear, the American Vice-President of Astroturf flies over from the USA with a new offer of £850k. He wants us to be the flagship for his new water-based surfaces in this country and is prepared to see us as a loss-leader in this context.

In the last two weeks we have appointed ten new members of staff for September, in the course of which process various senior members of staff and I have interviewed nearly forty candidates. Today it was Food Technology—only someone who was tired of living would have the nerve to call it 'Cooking' these days. I offer the post to our preferred candidate who tells me she would love to accept, but that she has agreed on the phone last night to accept a post at another school. So why did she come to see us today?

'I wanted to see Millfield and didn't think I'd get the job.'

I leave it to her and the other Head to work it out and to let me know her position within twenty-four hours. Later the other Head calls me. Neither he nor I have ever been in this position before, and I feel for him. He, poor chap, just cannot win and it's very galling for him. Either he agrees to release her from her verbal acceptance and has to start the recruiting task all over again, or else he does not release her, and hires someone who, from the outset, would prefer to be somewhere else. He decides on the former course, as I would have done, and we are lucky to get a first rate person for our job.

It is encouraging to know from time to time that parents do appreciate that tutors generally, and houseparents in particular, know a thing or two about how to handle the young. David and Barbara Agutter have received a letter thanking them for their 'patience and fortitude in the middle of a sea of hormones.'

With our chaplain, Simon, still confined to a wheel-chair, which he wishes was a proper Bath chair, Gwynne kindly took the Sunday service today in his place. It is Passion Sunday and she speaks with the passion of a true believer to the boys of St. Anne's and those girls from Acacia who are not involved in the sponsored swim. Very appositely, the subject of her address is Suffering, and therefore not unnaturally she mentions the word a good deal. Suddenly I am aware that the St Anne's boys are convulsed with that particularly virulent strain of silent laughter that can, *in extremis*, hasten cardiac arrest. The reason for their mute hilarity is what is going on in the front row, where David Trevis, their housemaster, is sitting with his 2-year-old son on his lap. Of all of us in the chapel, it is David who at that moment knows most about Suffering, for the little boy is whiling away the sermon by pulling clumps of his stoical father's hair out by the roots.

The Times gossip columnist now has his claws into us, following my letter of complaint earlier in the term. It leads this week with, 'In the Kremlin, the name of Millfield wafts around like the vapours of a bad vodka.' This is in the wake of the news that Mr Chubais (Alexi's father) has been promoted, and that Mr Yumashev (Polina's father) will now fill his place as chief of staff in the Kremlin. The moral is, I suppose, that it never pays to try to stand in the way of a juggernaut like a national newspaper. They have ways of punishing you for your temerity.

William Louey comes out from Hong Kong to visit his five Beijing protégés. His grandfather founded the island's bus and tram service and he describes himself as a rich kid who needs to put something back into society. He is a splendid, loquacious enthusiast who is plainly thrilled to see the youngsters' rapidly developing confidence. They are certainly a great credit to him, and have all picked up and acted on his insistence that they enter the lists on all fronts here, and that their widest development is important, not merely their academic success. I really like his no-nonsense approach. If only all billionaires were like this!

A bright boy from Hanoi has got himself into a bit of trouble, and the harder we try to throw him ropes to extricate him from the hole he has dug for himself, the harder he keeps digging. It boils down to the fact that he has been pestering and frightening younger boys in his House. He is warned off, but is it bullying or cultural misunderstanding? We are all aware that he has not been home for a year and a half and we can sympathize with his sense of dislocation. But then he goes back to the others and the whole thing starts again. I decide to put him in the sixth-form House next term, so that the problem cannot recur, and arrange to see him to explain this to him. I had expected deference and acceptance of the position, I admit, and am surprised therefore to find him defiant. He argues, weeps, talks of his honour. I write to him afterwards to try to reassure him that the move is for the best, only to learn that he has been back to the younger boys yet again to try to get them to change their story.

It's the first day of the Easter holiday and Julia and I go round to see Steve Wallis, our colleague, who is desperately weakened by the cancer that has afflicted him since the start of the school year. He was one of the most dynamic of teachers, a fine mathematician and arguably an even better rugby coach. None of us will forget watching the way in which he would get perhaps sixty boys and five other tutors organized on rugby skills on the junior pitch for a couple of hours at a stretch without flagging. Now he is much reduced, though his interest in the school is undimmed. Neither of us knew that this would be our last sight of him. Steve died later in the month, while we were in the Far East on a recruiting tour. Later, we dedicated his old classroom to him and planted a tree by the Jubilee pitch in his memory.

This year, the tour schedule took in Jakarta, Brunei, Singapore, Malaysia, Hong Kong and Beijing. I interviewed over thirty prospective pupils, spoke at reunions in each centre, and met many old friends. There was a memorable meeting in Brunei with the Minister for Education, Pehan Aziz. I was ushered in at one door, as an earlier visitor was ushered out of another. It turned out that this had been the Minister for Education in Iran, and Pehan Aziz was in a state of some shock.

'He lectured me about having a female secretary. Apparently in Iran women may not even drive a car.'

He was generous in his praise of our role in the education of the next generation of young Bruneians, 'We provide the ingredients but you are the cook.'

In Beijing, we arrived to find that we had the first afternoon free, so we asked the concierge in our hotel how long it would take to the city centre. He said about twenty-five minutes, and we set off along the vast boulevards with a spring in our step to match the bright spring weather. We kept going past chess players, bird sellers, girls playing cards on the pavement, peach blossom, kites, thousands of leisurely cyclists and old men doing their Tai Chi. We only went wrong once when the map suggested we could go through what looked like a park but turned out to be a clinic. This was confirmed by the fact that everyone was wearing pyjamas. We attracted plenty of attention, and indeed saw only two other long-nosed folk all afternoon. For this is what differentiates us, in the Chinese mind. My nose, distinctive at any time, gave thousands of Beijing residents immense pleasure. But it was fully four hours before we eventually staggered into Tiananmen Square. Once back in the hotel, I asked the concierge why he had thought twenty-five minutes sufficient for the walk.

'Walk?' he said, 'No one has walked before. I thought you'd go by taxi.'

The next morning, I interviewed nine pupils from Number 4 School and from the school attached to the People's University. They were all top students, all idealistic and very aware of their parents' lost education, which had coincided with the Cultural Revolution. Their English was remarkably good, even though they were all specialist scientists and mathematicians. One of the pupils talked about his recent project entitled, 'How to clean rabbits and keep city good.' Initial confusion evaporated when it became clear that 'rabbits' were really 'rubbish'. His commitment to his cause was deeply impressive.

On the first day of term, we have 1,248 youngsters all safely returned, bar one Thai boy who has done a runner and frightens everyone to death. Eventually he is discovered in Cheltenham holed up with a compatriot, who rejoices in the name Turdrat. Kate has returned, but there is a lot less of her than there was when we said goodbye last month. She has lost three kilos in her mother's care, in the teeth of an immense amount of discussion concerning her eating-disordered state. She has to turn round and return home immediately, until she can meet the weight targets set out in black-and-white for her weeks ago. This will unleash a storm of parental fury. Mother is as tall as me and assures me she weighed only seven stone when she was married, so she is not easily persuaded that her daughter is in a danger zone.

It's the end of a six week General Election campaign, and the local Natural Law candidate has come up with a real vote winner. She wants to inflict on the Armed Services compulsory classes in transcendental meditation. The Army, it seems, must march on its mantra. I put the suggestion to my General Studies class to see what reactions it would get. The first query seemed to summarize the prevailing view. 'I wonder how that would square with bayonet drill?'

Something entirely new happens every day. This afternoon, a tutor came across a third-year boy alone on the gallery in the swimming pool masturbating. He was in full view of anyone looking up from outside, but fled when he realized he had been seen. His mother is waiting for him downstairs, and so the tutor tells her about what he has just observed. She bursts out laughing and plays the incident down in a way which is itself distressing. Can this be her honest reaction? Thankfully the boy was not discovered by another pupil, for he would probably not have been allowed to forget it in a hurry. The matter will be referred to the counsellor. The act itself is not significant, of course, but its semi-public performance certainly is.

Suddenly three girls are confirmed as suffering from bulimia. All are boarders and each is starting to have a disturbing influence on those around her. We know the dreadful impact this wretched condition can have on others. It can go through a House like a virus, with the younger girls keen to emulate their seniors, in this as in other respects. The deception, the lies, the pressure applied to others not to tell on their friends—all this conspires to corrode the mutual trust necessary to happy life in a boarding house, as in any home. I have no compunction, therefore, about requiring them each to leave until we can be convinced that they are able to beat the habit. Understandably the air waves fill up with dismay, for these are three bright, popular, outstanding people in their GCSE year whom we will all miss. Colleagues, friends, parents all urge a more relaxed line, but having heard the *cris de coeur* from the others in their Houses, this is not possible. The only sickening part of it all is when psychiatrists start weighing in at parental request, and expense I imagine, even though they have no personal knowledge of the girls or of the context in which they need to live and work here. It's the usual story: all those with special pleading only have one side of the equation, whereas I am burdened with both.

Today we appointed our seventeenth full-time teacher for next year and there are still two more to go. When I mention this to other Heads they assume we have had a mass walk-out, but forget that we have a full complement of 190 full-time teachers, not counting the coaching staff. Only the Physics job has given us any real difficulty so far. All the others have produced short-lists of well qualified, enthusiastic people, especially among newly qualified teachers, brimful of professional and personal zeal. If I were to apply for these posts myself, I wouldn't get a look in nowadays. One applicant has coaching qualifications in fourteen sports, in addition of course to his academic degree. Another is a hockey international, a third has conducted a soccer coaching session in front of 78,000 people in the Rose Bowl in California, and so on. But eighty interviews, on top of everything else, take a lot of time. Thus on two mornings this week I've had ten and eleven meetings in the diary before lunch.

In the post today are letters from two people who appear to have lost their marbles. The first is from a PE teacher from a school in Plymouth. He brought some swimmers here recently and stubbed his toe on the steps in the gallery. He has not been prevented from getting to work by his injury but is clearly trying on some spurious insurance claim and is anxious to imply that we are responsible for his injury. The second is from a prospective parent who is complaining that we don't offer weekly boarding. We have never offered weekly boarding and have never claimed to offer it. Nevertheless, she is incensed. 'I have spent seventeen years in Asia and have returned to Surrey now to be near my children.' So naturally she wants to send them to school in Somerset.

This Sunday we held our first Millfield Challenge day, the brain child of the Tutor for Admissions, Richard Woodhead. We had twelve teams of boys and girls from prep schools throughout the South West, plus their supporters. There were team tasks in the pool, orienteering, river crossings—all physically and mentally demanding stuff. The youngsters took no prisoners. A more competitive bunch it would be hard to imagine. My favourite exchange was with a small boy, puffing like a steam train and puce in the face, lying by the bridge.

'Have you finished already?'

'No, Sir. I've just been to the toilet.'

A horse, trained as an eventer and thus skilled at clearing obstacles, decided to jump the hedge from its field into the Somerton Road this afternoon. It careered across the main road into Portway, then took a sharp turn right down our road, past our house, and skidded to a halt at the end, where it ate all our neighbour's roses. He eventually collared the wretched animal, which was returned to school under close arrest where it was presumably put on iron rations to curb its wanderlust. No injury or deaths on the main road. No traffic accident. Very lucky. But it will cost me a bottle or two of wine to placate our kind neighbour.

Alan Lerwill, who will teach PE and be our senior athletics coach next term, came down to watch our House Athletics finals. He was not disappointed.

'It's a far higher standard than the county finals,' he said.

Carl threw the weight out of the arena, achieving a new British Junior record and a number of already impressive school records were broken, cheered by the whole school who were in good spirits, stretched out on the grassy bank in the sunshine overlooking the track.

The sculpture project by Charlie Hadcock has now arrived. It's a large cast iron version of his original polystyrene packing cases, observing the Golden Ratio, on which Charlie will talk to the pupils—or anyone else—at the drop of a hat. He quotes Vetruvius from the fifth century BC, 'The definition of good architecture is that it does not claim more of the space we all share than it should.' It will go in the quad and be wonderfully controversial.

We have won a third consecutive senior water polo match, where conditions were described in the match report as 'wet under foot.'

The following day we opened the new Rainbow squash courts. After an impressive junior tournament, there was an exhibition match, introduced by our coach, Jonah Barrington. This was between Peter Marshall, the former UK top string, and Simon

Parke, currently fourth in the world. Both are in their mid-twenties, both are Jonah's protégés and both have suffered two years of serious illness, from which they have now almost recovered. It was enthralling: a titanic battle between two friends who happen to be very evenly matched. I counted over fifty shots in one point alone. Our people certainly had a glimpse of something approaching perfection today.

A note from a Head of Year. 'Alison, at Grange, found in possession of fireworks. Claims she did not know the word "banger" meant firework—a perfectly understandable error. She thought they were sausages. One week school gating.'

Over dinner with the headmaster of King's College Taunton, Simon Funnell, I expose my lamentable ignorance of golf when claiming to have been visited recently by none other than the golf champion Derek Woosnam. The next day I get a fax from Simon, purporting to come from the *Daily Telegraph*: 'Top Public School admits Arbuthnot Woosnam, son of famous golfer Derek. At Millfield, he will join the sons of other top sportsmen, including Arthur Bruno, Harold Lineker and Cyril Faldo.'

A GCSE candidate is found in an exam with five words written on his hand. The Exam Board will be notified, but in case they are lenient, the boy is allowed to continue his exam once he has been taken out of the exam hall to have the offending words washed off. It is only later that we realize that the Board's rubric for such cases states that 'evidence of improper conduct must be submitted to the Board.' It's lucky for the boy that we do not live in Iran.

At the end of a busy half-term, I get a report from Claire, our counsellor, currently beset by girls with eating disorders, headed 'A day in the life of your counsellor, aged 56¾ and ageing.'

This morning my General Studies class trooped out in high spirits, singing the Marseillaise—I forget why that had suddenly become relevant in my class—to find the King of Oman, his wife Mme Gerda and Taimur their son waiting outside. They are right up to date on the Rio +5 agenda and indeed on all green issues. We seem to spend more time talking about such things than we do about Taimur's entry—such a break to be able to assume that parents are on your side from the outset, to the point where they feel able to discuss their other interests instead of just cracking up their children. Nicer for the children, too. I'd really like to invite him to speak to our sixth-form, but geography rules it out sadly.

An unhappy start to a fine Saturday morning. I have to suspend a boy who has, for some inexplicable reason, fed gin to his horse. He has offered no compelling clue to explain his actions: 'I just thought it was a good idea at the time.'

I cheer myself up in the afternoon by seeing Ralph Dorey score 170 against the Free Foresters, and the opening pair of the Foals C side scoring 245 not out against Downside's A team.

A team of nine people have come over from Renong in Malaysia to spend a couple of days learning in detail how Millfield works. This is the latest in a series of meetings, here and in Kuala Lumpur, exploring the possibility of our becoming the model for their proposed sixth-form college, to be built on a one hundred acre site cleared especially for the purpose. Renong is one of the biggest and most reputable commercial outfits in Malaysia, and at my meeting with their CEO, Tan Sri Halim, during my Easter trip, he had expressed enthusiasm for the project. The prospect has enormous implications for us, involving as it would, the initial provision of senior staff and academic advisers. There are even long-term possibilities of being able to offer our staff a year's experience in the college as part of their continuous professional development. This would, I think, be a unique development and one that attracts me greatly to the proposal.

When they arrive, our guests are welcomed and immediately embark on a cycle of agreed meetings with a couple of dozen colleagues who all realize fully what is at stake here. As the programme unwinds, however, we become increasingly aware that their level of interest in what we have to show them and discuss with them is disappointingly low. Indeed, references to shopping in Clark's Village start to surface and we all begin to question their motivation. By the end of day two, their credibility as a fact-finding team is shot, and we see them off with mixed feelings in their two posh vehicles, crammed with booty from the local shoe shops.

I write to try to lay out the next steps in this collaborative venture, which we still hope may be on track, and for weeks receive no reply. Then quite by chance, talking with James Sabben-Clare, the headmaster of Winchester, it dawns on me that not only have Renong gone with Winchester in this joint venture, but that they had agreed to do so even before their team visited us. Our two schools could, of course, hardly be more different, and since they were looking for a co-educational college, their decision to go ultimately with a single sex school seems perverse. We have been taken for a ride, and much staff time and energy has been gratuitously wasted. It is now clear that shopping was indeed the sole purpose of their trip to Street. I write a recriminatory letter, but have, of course, never heard from them again.

George, a sixth-former whom we would all see as a pillar of the community, has written a note of pure desolation to his group tutor. He has found himself weeping openly in class and in the quad, to the distress of friends and teachers, who are at a loss how to help him. I insist that he be collected by his father, even though George does not wish to contact him. Eventually he comes in and has a three-hour meeting with our counsellor. She recommends psychological help, but the father, a successful surgeon, refuses point blank, because of the stigma he feels would attach to this among his professional colleagues.

It is Mencap day, one of the best days in our calendar. Some 800 people with learning difficulties and their carers converge on the school from all over the south west. The staff and pupils are there in force to welcome them and to engage them throughout the day in all the activities we can dream up all over our campus. As usual, I am lost in admiration for the way our people deploy limitless patience in helping others to achieve unfamiliar things, and for our guests' incomparable determination to achieve them. They are not deterred by initial failure. It's a lesson for us all. Andy in the gym is teaching one young man how to score at basketball. Bounce, bounce, bounce and throw. Three hours later when I return they are still at it. And Boris, who does not give much away as a rule, spends well over an hour with a young woman who is clearly smitten with him, encouraging her to hit a badminton shuttle over the net. Our girls accept with grace the unexpected warmth of our guests' embraces. But best of all is seeing the way in which those of our people whose records here are not entirely unblemished respond with such genuine pleasure to their charges' successes. Asked to do something whose importance they can appreciate, the young invariably respond positively, it seems.

People seem to have realized that I am retiring, but assume— hope?—that it's this year. A parent came up to me in Street yesterday and said, without intended irony, I think, 'Are you still alive?'

At four o'clock this afternoon, I had a family from Hong Kong, a young Moldavian girl, and a German family in my room, talking about prospective entry, when to my embarrassment sounds of raised voices, even thumps as in fighting break out right underneath my window from the Bolts. I smile wanly and try to explain it all in terms of end-of-term high spirits. Later, I make enquiries, and discover that it all came from a scheduled activity in role play. This week's theme was 'Aggression.'

Mrs P. arrives in my room, unannounced, with her entire family, comprising five and seven-ninths children, one of whom is with us. He has been involved in a fight in his House and has lost a tooth. Sadly, it transpires that this is the same tooth that was fixed at great expense very recently. Mother, heavily pregnant, is furious and it's easy to see why. One can make all sorts of allowances for anyone in her current state, especially when she is confronted by renewed expense and what looks like an unprovoked attack by another boy. However, she quickly becomes hysterical, and from then on there's no possibility of getting to the bottom of things. She is going to take out a prosecution for assault on the other boy. I know this chap quite well, and find it hard to see him as a natural aggressor. Mrs P. has no doubt at all, however.

'My son has told me everything. He never lies. It was an entirely unprovoked assault.'

She tells me repeatedly that she is a born-again Christian, but in this case she wants a tooth for a tooth. She has spent three hours on the phone to her son's long-suffering houseparents and expresses amazement when I tell her that she has reduced her housemother to tears. She assures me that she has written a six page letter of complaint to me about the 'fact' that we have a more relaxed disciplinary policy for the sons of the wealthy than for those of more modest means. I try to tell her it's bunkum but she is utterly sure of herself. She will come back for a pound of flesh tomorrow.

Tomorrow dawns, and the post brings her letter, as threatened, which thuds on to my desk along with the report of the investigation into the incident. Thus I am well prepared for her subsequent visit. It is now clear that her son-who-never-lies (how often have I heard that from parents?) had been making a string of racist remarks at his aggressor until patience had snapped and the blow was landed. Her wretched son admits it, and his poor mother implodes. From a position of incontrovertible rectitude to one of abject apology is a hard journey for anyone, and by the end I feel for her. Her hapless son deserves all that she is undoubtedly going to give him.

Alex White is thirteen, Head Boy of Millfield Preparatory School. He starts his end-of-term speech to a dauntingly large audience of parents and friends on a splendidly confident note: 'As Henry VIII said to his six wives, I shan't keep you long.'

Ivan has been involved in a number of nasty incidents, all of which cumulatively point to the fact that he is one of those rarities—a nasty piece of work. On Parents' Day, at eight in the morning, as two or three thousand people start to gather outside, and when I should be out there with them, I spend an hour with the entire family. They are over from Europe to see me, and I have to try to get his decent father to understand that his son is not the Archangel Gabriel. Difficult at any time, but much harder when his doting mother, his grandparents and his siblings are all there as a sort of mute audience. Ivan reveals himself as the spoilt, manipulative boy we know him to be, but his barefaced lies do shock me nevertheless. With complete confidence, and with his parents' support, he tries to shift the blame for his unacceptable actions—bullying, stealing, defiance—by putting up a smoke screen of outrageous allegations about a whole range of colleagues. But he doesn't stop there. The whole school is at fault. Only when they are in trouble do people resort to allegations about the whole school being drunk and permanently on drugs. He says all this without batting an eyelid. I shall not allow him back; he has a deeply baleful impact on others.

Later that day, Ralph Clark, the retiring Chairman of Governors, is presented with a bronze miniature of the Henry Moore sculpture in front of 2,500 people. He had helped to acquire the original for Street in the first place, and its departure to the USA was naturally painful to him. This, then, was a welcome gesture of Millfield's indebtedness to him for many years of service to the school. Among other things which I try to cram into my speech, I have to say goodbye to 350 senior pupils and 23 full-time staff. Of these, the nine who are retiring have between them clocked up over 200 years of service to the school. These are always emotionally charged times for the leavers, and later, over tea on the lawns, everyone is in floods of tears. Gerry Wilson is given a great send off after his thirty-seven years as our chief cricket coach. The affection shown for him is well earned. He has helped a handful of players into national sides, over twenty players into county cricket sides, and hundreds into good club sides. The fact that in two days time we are for the third year running in the final of the Lord's Taverners Trophy is in large part down to him.

That evening, lying prone at home, drained, with a box of sweets from Mrs Ahuja, I hear the phone ring. It's the athletes on their way home from the National Athletics finals at Abingdon to tell me that the boys won and the girls were third, from thousands of initial entries. It's hard to imagine a better end to a big day. We seem also to have won the independent schools' Youll tennis cup for the second time in two years. This is a record for us, but I suppose that's because we have only been allowed to participate in the competition for two years.

Among the August letters this year is a surprisingly large group of requests from the parents of pupils who have done better than expected. They write as a consequence of this to ask for bursaries for their children. Some are insistent, some aggressive even, and none seem to recognize the amazing cheek they have in making any such request at all, let alone when made a week or so before the start date for funds which were budgeted a year ago and deployed in February when the gathered field of applicants was considered. And in any case, could they not see that a large part of the unexpectedly high standards achieved by their offspring is down to the devoted teaching they have received here?

Chapter 7

Madam Millfield proves elusive

SEPTEMBER 1997. The first day of my last year in employment. BBC TV marks it by making a documentary drama of the arrest here of Paul Hickson, leading to his conviction for a rape committed in a previous existence. This includes an interview with me, about which I have grave misgivings. Yet if you don't take part, it is made to look as if you have something to hide.

The arrival of Nigel Mansell, with his son Leo, allows us all to change up a gear, as it were. We had thought to ask him if we could photograph him at the wheel of our new golf buggy, in which visitors are to be toured around the campus in future, but decided eventually that it would really be a bit tacky. They are a well-knit family and we all enjoy their visit, as I think do they. Leo says at one stage, almost to himself, 'I really like this place. All the other schools I've been to, well, it's like being in church all the time.' I did not ask which ones he had in mind but I can probably guess.

Princess Diana's funeral seems to leave most of us pretty unmoved, yet to my sadness I seem to have lost a friend over it. Looking round the kitchens just before the start of term, I ask one long-serving assistant how she is. She looks at me in anguish.

'Isn't it awful!' she says.

'What is?' I ask, genuinely alarmed for her and fearing some family catastrophe.

'Why, the Princess's death.'

I was so relieved that, tactlessly, I just laughed. If looks could kill, I'd be dead as a doornail. In fact, as things turned out, she never spoke a word to me again, and though I apologized profusely, she was unable to forgive me for my insensitivity. From this, I learnt something about Diana's effect on people, if nothing about Diana.

Ben is a pupil in Shapwick House, where Boris is. It seems that his aunt has been taken hostage in Chechnya, and the release price is said to be £2 million. He is greatly upset by this. The PM is engaged in discussions with the FCO. Presumably if the abductors knew of the Yeltsin connection, they would double their ransom demand. Or perhaps they did know!

This term, we are admitting 387 new pupils and are welcoming 23 new tutors. There are now forty-five tutors under the age of thirty in the school, among whom I think I can see five or six future headteachers, if that's the route they want to take in due course. We have two new water-based Astro hockey pitches, which make us the best venue in the country for hockey festivals. We have Speakeasy—a voice-mail box for every pupil. We have entirely new library arrangements. Oh, and we have a solarium in the stables to keep our horses warm. The staff will want one next. And the new arrangements for girls' dress seem to work tolerably well. They have to wear a jacket and trousers or skirt—a choice of three colours—and so of course they all turn up in black.

One new pupil arrives at Millfield House from Kuala Lumpur, finds that he is sharing with another boy, and asks the taxi driver to take him to another school. Luckily the housemaster manages to persuade him that it's too late at night to be sure of another place elsewhere and that his best plan is to stay with us at least until morning. This works well. By morning the poor chap has recovered to the point where he is willing to give us, and his room-mate, a chance, and he winds up settling in very well.

The first day of term is the first day of our grand-daughter Nell's first school year and the first day also of my last. I feel absurdly proud of this, having reconciled myself to the fact that there is a fifty-seven-year gap between us.

A little 13-year-old boy refuses to join his House, Orchards. To convince his father of the depth of his conviction on this issue, he lies down in front of his father's car outside the House and refuses to budge. Wisely his father decides to take him home again and try a different, more persuasive tack. I think he had a hint that his son meant business when earlier in the day the boy had let down all four car tyres.

The headmaster of Winchester rings me. The Yeltsins are exploring a place there for Boris for this term. Surprisingly it seems that they are able to find a place for him! There has been no contact with us over any proposed move, but it may have something to do with the fact that Winchester came top in the summer's league tables. I can just hear grandfather Yeltsin asking pointedly why his grandson is not in the top school in the UK. The next day, Tanya Yeltsin and Alex make a special trip to Millfield to explain their position. I appreciate very much the fact that they want to do this in person. They are full of praise for Millfield but express interest in Winchester as a 'different kind of school for Boris.' If it's difference they want, they won't be disappointed.

Four days in, and we have lost no one yet, though there have been some close shaves. A call from New York, for instance: 'My daughter feels out of her depth. Should I take her out?' No, give her time. It cannot be good for her to encourage her to run for cover at the first sign of difficulty. Or another call from Kiev, 'My son feels he has no friends. I want to withdraw him.' Investigations reveal that he has been swanking that he is the Ukrainian skateboarding champion, but that his story is blown when he refuses to mount a skateboard. Hence his unhappiness.

But the weather is fine and the tears of those who feel bereft are beginning to dry, thanks to the efforts of the House staff and the counsellors, whose diaries have been very full this far. I recall my first term ever, when a delightful sixth-form girl came to see me after just a week and said that, regrettably, she was going to have to return to her home in Cardiff.

'But why?' I asked, wracked with guilt that things had already not worked out.

'Well, you see,' she said, 'It's just that my boyfriend lives with my mother and I don't trust her with him.'

Game, set and match.

The new Astro pitches are christened with a 2nd XI match against Shepton Mallet at 3.0 p.m. on Saturday 13th September and our first goal is scored seven minutes later. At that precise moment, a particularly strong gust of wind—part of the prevailing gale—blew all the corner flags down. The rending of the veil? An omen? Probably just a gust of wind. The next match sees the girls in action on the same pitch. At half-time, they retire to their goal to get their pep-talk, and the water hoses are switched on to give the surface its necessary dousing. Unfortunately, the hoses have not been properly aligned and a substantial jet of cold water is aimed straight at the goal where our team is huddled, soaking them all to the bone. Fortunately our girls rock with laughter. It is a moment to treasure, partly because of the cock-up, of course, but also for their reaction. This must be part of the reason why I would so much rather watch them playing than any bunch of grimly competitive professional players.

The first week is always punctuated with my Headmaster's Assemblies. I tear up the usual fistful of notes shortly before the first and decide to talk about Lyndon Johnson's Head Start programme for four-to-six-year olds in the States thirty years ago, to illustrate some thoughts on the question 'Can intelligence be taught?' I figure this should be an encouraging theme for everyone to start a new academic year with, bearing in mind the range of ability we have and the very special difficulties that so many of them have to struggle to overcome in their studies. I mention that I may be the only headteacher in the UK to have failed the eleven-plus exam. Should I be upset that nobody seems surprised?

And to the Upper Sixth I talk about bees, communities, reciprocity, and the will of the many prevailing over the despotism of each. I end with two of my favourite epitaphs, which seemed appropriate at the time.

Hier ruhen meine Gebeine,
ich wollt' es wären Deine. (Heinrich Heine)
And the tombstone in Elgin Cathedral.
Here lie I, Martin Elginbrodde:
Hae mercy o' my soul, Lord God,
As I wad do, were I Lord God,
And ye were Martin Elginbrodde.

Sarah, in her first week here, has inflicted twenty-eight bruises on her room-mate, as counted by the school doctor. She has fantasized endlessly in the House about expulsion, drugs, abuse and her family, and has caused havoc among the other girls. I tell her poor, despairing mother that I cannot re-admit her as a boarder. The mother pulls out all the stops on her daughter's behalf.

'It's only two weeks since Princess Diana died. It's profoundly affected her.' I can sympathize with parental anguish, but this....

A quad from the housemaster of Alexei Kisselev, the 13-year-old son of a big Russian television presenter, 'Alexei, new this term, was a real problem during the House song rehearsal. He was offering money to the girls round him for oral sex.' We do have an eclectic bunch here. No wonder he's already known as Kissalot.

Xiao Baoquiang, one of the three new Beijing scholars, was playing on the golf course today and struck a good shot. His tutor, who was passing, congratulated him and suggested that he had obviously played before.

'Yes, I have,' said Xiao, 'Yesterday.'

Which, it transpires, was the first time he'd held a golf club.

Bow, as the boys call him, confused his tutor with his housemaster in the House last night, and immediately apologized, 'All you Westerners look alike to me, I'm afraid.'

A Mexican mother has responded to a tearful phone call from her 13-year-old son by flying over to remove him. By the time she arrived, of course, the boy had established himself and wanted to stay. The father, separated and watching this impotently from the sidelines, is distraught on the phone and has my complete sympathy. The mother, on the other hand, realizes she is now acting in her own interests alone, rather than her son's, but says lamely that she is son-sick and cannot be without him. She takes him home with her, to our dismay, for he is a most likeable chap who would have fitted in very well here.

I met an identical pair of bishops, the Right Reverends Michael and Peter Ball who, to my delight, have moved into the area. On the back of a card they gave me with their new address, Michael had written, 'I cheated in my metaphysics exam. I looked into the soul of the boy sitting next to me.'

Two weeks into the term and Alexei Kissalev has already developed an unhealthily high profile. When reprimanded by a teacher, he said darkly, 'In Russia, people are shot for talking to me like that.'

The next day, he was found laying heavy bets during a PE lesson on whether someone could do ten press-ups. All this on top of his sexual invitations during the House song suggests he is not long for our world.

Sunday chapel. The Lord's prayer. A telephone rings and a new Thai boy leaps out and down the stairs, clutching his mobile—the first time this instrument has been used as a reason for premature escape from chapel. It probably won't be the last unless we do something serious about mobiles, which are beginning to infiltrate the campus in unacceptable ways.

At an HMC Committee meeting, we are discussing unity with the Girls' Schools Association. Their President announces appositely at one point, 'You cannot amalgamate with us unilaterally.'

On the same day that a Miss Foal applies for the post of Director of Riding I read that President Banana of Zimbabwe has been charged with sodomy.

Alexei is filling my in-tray. Quads are arriving in profusion every day now. 'He had a headache in class so I sent him to the medical centre. They sent him back, but instead of returning to class, he phoned his mother in Moscow. When I remonstrated, he said he had a right to phone home if he was dying. I find him utterly exasperating.'

Two new 13-year-old boys have emerged as problems on an epic scale already. They wrote down their room-mate's PIN number, swiped his card, withdrew the most money they could from the hole in the wall, split the loot and burnt the card. A serious crime. One parent, confronted by this situation, declared dogmatically, 'My son is incapable of such action.' But the boy has confessed. Given the number of witnesses at each stage, he had no choice but to do so.

The House which, more than any other recently, has been afflicted by a series of eating disorders, has chosen as their song for the House competition 'Food, glorious food.'

Mr S. calls from Kansas, at 3 a.m. his time, to defend his son, who has had a positive drug test. Father owns and hires Boeing 747s, is fabulously wealthy and is used to getting his way. Later in the morning, Mrs B. comes to see me about her daughter. Her husband has left them to go and live in San Diego and they are practically destitute, on social security. Could any two parents illustrate more vividly the extraordinary range of financial backing available to youngsters here.

We are being inspected this week. There are seventeen inspectors looking at every angle of our operation for five days. At the end of the first day, all seems to be going quite well, and I am touched by those pupils and colleagues who express anxiety that the whole exercise may be affecting my life span. I feel ridiculously proud of the school, however, and thus positively relish the interest the inspectors take in us.

The 4th XV have decided to call themselves the Neanderthals this year and seem to be surprised that other teams with scheduled fixtures appear to be cancelling matches with them, possibly out of sheer fright. To help drum up some opposition for them, I suggested they should call themselves the Fairies instead, but they turned down my idea.

Two Thai brothers have given up golf already. Why?

'Because it's too tiring, Sir.'

'But you've played plenty of golf before.'

'Yes, Sir, but only with a buggy or a caddy. Here you have to walk *and* carry your clubs at the same time, all by yourself.'

Eric Jones was being inspected in his chemistry laboratory when the inspector drew his attention to smoke rising from the waste-paper basket. Incinerating a class is not always the best way to endear oneself to an inspector, so after the class Eric sought out the inspector in the Staff Room to offer him coffee and make amends. Sadly, he poured water from the cold kettle, and did not realize this until later when he tasted his own coffee. 'A flaming good lesson, though,' he added bravely.

The inspection is over. HMC's first five-day affair, and our seventeen guests have departed. With perhaps just one exception they were superbly supportive, helpful, sympathetic, perceptive and professional: we were lucky to have had them. The report is a good one with just five minor recommendations. One comment from a departing inspector thrilled me: 'The staff just never give up on the kids.' Exactly! We had a good post-inspection bash in the staff room afterwards with twenty entries for my limerick competition on the thrills and spills of being inspected. The next day, Saturday, at 8 a.m.

[112]

we got down to the business of analysing the recommended action points arising from the oral report—a process only interrupted by my need to open the English Schools' Team Swimming Championships in the pool in the afternoon. Over 500 schools had entered, and we had a team in every one of the eight finals. We won five of them with four records. A really good day.

On the advice of the Maths Department, I watched a programme on Fermat's Last Theorem. Fermat was a mathematician, who in 1637 conjectured that $x3 + y3 = z3$, but left no proof that this was so. For 300 years, other mathematicians struggled in vain to prove the theorem. Then Professor Andrew Wiles, from Cambridge, spent seven years on it, and solved it. Why was I so entranced by the programme when I understood nothing of the task he had set himself? Perhaps it was just a sense of awe that the human brain can devote itself so single-mindedly to a theory which, on the face of it, has no intrinsic practical outcome at all. It reminds me of Fran Lebowitz' dictum: 'Stand firm in your refusal to remain conscious during algebra. In real life, I assure you, there is no such thing as algebra.'

So far, Alexei has confined himself to betting, sexual invitations and threatening staff. To date he has blandly denied everything, adopting a tone of mild, urbane indignation that we should see him in anything other than a favourable light. Now however he has started bullying other boys, and more sinister yet, has been getting a couple of other Russian boys, over whom he seems to have some influence, to do the bullying for him. He has been here less than a month but I have now suspended him and invited his parents to come over to discuss the conditions of his return. His poor housemaster at Etonhurst has admitted that throughout yesterday's trip with two teams to Plymouth, when all the boys behaved in exemplary fashion—good company throughout, the bus driver impressed—he spent the entire time worrying about Alexei's baleful influence in the House. This cannot go on.

This has been some Saturday. A reunion lunch for some seventy Old Millfieldians, rugby against Blundell's, tennis against Repton, the last performance of the preparatory school's play in our theatre, and the chance to address 400 new parents of third-year boys. All this the day after the House song competition with 971 singers, triumphantly climaxing so many hours of rehearsals. Then, as the last parents left late in the afternoon, and I thought the day was coming to an end, the news of a serious fight came through. An investigation revealed that two Thai boys had assaulted two other Thais, one of whom wound up with a broken nose. They offered the flimsiest of excuses for the attack and remained entirely impassive throughout the enquiry, apparently genuinely unconcerned by what they had done, and indeed by the outcome. I have had to expel them both, with all the agonising phoning of families that this entails. The police were involved, and of course our medical services. Saturday evening, which was to have included a dinner party, was swallowed up by this extraordinary flare-up which, from start to finish, seems to make no sense at all.

Three Lower Sixth girls have been to see me to offer their services as counsellors for others who suffer from eating disorders, as they themselves have suffered earlier. It is not an easy proposition to accept, despite their obvious goodwill and wish to help others, as well as their own personal experience. They talk eagerly, almost voyeuristically about this complex and tantalisingly difficult condition, as if having 'been there—done that' was enough to qualify them in the front line of the war we are waging against such disorders. I'll talk to our professional counsellor about their possible involvement, but remain sceptical myself.

They are followed by two third-year boys, suspended in their first fortnight for stealing their friend's credit card. One of them shows no sign of remorse at all. He looks like real trouble. A rich, spoilt kid from Gstaad, who seems to have had everything fall into his lap so far in his short life. He's one of the very few people I find it really hard to like here.

A nice letter from Karachi.

Dear Mr Martin,

Our daughter, who is entered for Millfield in 2006, has passed with top marks from Form 1 to Form 2. Please find enclosed her progress report, which I think you will find is excellent.

I think the little girl in question is now four. I read the letter to staff with the assurance that, if she is promoted to Form 3, they will be the first to hear.

Julia and I visit a boarding house each week to spend the evening with the pupils in their natural habitat. Yesterday it was Orchards, the largest House, and one in which it is almost impossible to get round all sixty boys in just three hours. Yoshi, Neil and Phil Pote were all outside waiting for us at 7. 'Be welcome', shouts Neil in his characteristically irrepressible way. Even Edward managed a wan smile, which was encouraging since it was he who had flung himself in front of his father's car to prevent him driving him to school at the start of term.

Home at 11, and just time to ring an old friend, Richard Hamilton, whom I had not seen since my mother's funeral, to ask him to come and lecture on the voluntary sector here; and then Monty Saul to ask her to give away the prizes at the international chess competition we are due to host in a month or two. The next day in London, interviewing the Morehead scholarship applicants for the University of North Carolina, I run into the same Richard in Oxford Street. And then Monty comes and sits next to me on the train coming home, not realising I am her neighbour until she has sat down. I enjoy coincidences so much! I hope she does too!

John Grimshaw of Sustrans gives a compelling talk to the sixth-form on cycle power. He is an impressive missionary for cycle paths and associated sculpture. I show him our new cast-iron Charlie Hadcock sculpture, Golden Ratio, in the quad and he is impressed.

A third-former trots past on some mission and I ask him to join us and to let us know his opinion of the sculpture.

'It's nice,' he says non-committally.

'Nice,' says John. 'How can this be just nice?'

The small boy, who had plainly hardly noticed the piece before, having other preoccupations as small boys often do, studies us both warily and then gives the sculpture a really long, hard look. After a long silence, he declares with complete conviction, 'It's tremendous.'

At 9 this morning, after eighteen months, the final draft of our strategic plan lands with a thump on my desk. We've always known it would be a living, organic document, susceptible to change from the outset. But after John Grimshaw's visit, I am enthused by his suggestion that we should plan to construct a spur to the national cycle way from Street to Glastonbury across the levels. This could be a further £50,000 over three years, a sum which would diminish as we were successful in attracting subsidies. And this less than eight hours since the strategic plan was published. That's what I love most about Millfield. Nothing ever stays still for long.

My successor Peter and his wife Chrissie come for the night, for drinks, supper, soapbox in the Staff room, meetings with key people and tours of the games in the afternoon. They are excellent, talking with everyone with obvious glee and all is very well. But it is weird all the same, however hard I have tried to prepare for it, to realize how completely transparent I have suddenly become to colleagues and pupils who, quite rightly, must look to the future. I feel invisible.

Normally a Tuesday is not the busiest day of the week, but yesterday was an exception. And I hope it stays that way.

7.30 a.m. Phone call from Katayun in Bombay about her son.

8.00 The Deputy Headmaster as usual, staff problems and an affronted parent.

8.45 Pupils seeking advice on how to approach a tutor.

9.45 The Chairman of Governors of King's Taunton about my possible role there when I retire.

10.30 Two Heads of Year about Russian bullying.

11.00 Senior prefects, discussing money. A third-form boy has offered a £50 note in the tuck shop for crisps and they are rightly concerned.

11.30 An assistant house tutor about her own housing arrangements.

12.00 p.m. A rugby coach to discuss our teams' attitude in defeat and how it can be improved.

12.15 A question and answer session in the theatre with the prep school senior year.

12.45 Robert Baker, Ernie Els's coach, to discuss the proposed Millfield Golf Academy.

1.15 Heads of Year, lunch time discussion on use of the theatre foyer and how to handle recent abuse from boys from a host school on Saturday during our match there.

2.00 The counsellor to discuss two boys with bruised confidence.

2.15 A young tutor to receive an oral warning for striking two boys whom he had— rightly—separated in a fracas.

2.30 The chaplain with news of two unhappy tutors.

3.00 The Director of Studies with a range of curricular matters to get to grips with.

3.45 Three sets of prospective parents in a group to discuss their impressions of the school.

4.30 The Head of Maths, whom I had asked to head a group to discuss the shape of Parents' Day.

5.00 Laura Stamp, a governor of a school in Bangkok, to discuss possible links.

5.45 A young couple to talk through their aspirations to become houseparents.

6.15 A long phone call with a distressed mother who claims she is physically abused by her husband and is anxious for the children.

6.30–9.00 The Upper Sixth recital in the theatre. Wonderful indulgence after a full day, hearing nearly all my favourite musicians in action. Balm to the soul!

A week sailing in the Eastern Mediterranean over half-term has refreshed those parts of me that other holidays don't reach, and I feel ready for the fray again. How better to start back than with a meeting over lunch with eight Lower Sixth girls led by Bev and Anna, bubbling with ideas about how to launch the Green Council again. Litter collection, beach clearance, the construction of a windmill, fund-raising for Nepal, all this and more comes out in a stream of enthusiasm that is a joy to behold. Then straight off to Taunton to represent the school at a meeting for thirty Heads with the Social Services Department. What a contrast this proved to be to the meeting I'd just left! Here there was no animation, no agenda, no objectives, no outcome apparent or even sought, just a disorganized 'sharing of views' on inspections which we all felt had in any case already achieved their goals.

The HMC South West Divisional meeting. One speaker has come to air the question of stress. I sense that I may be slow on the uptake with this issue, but I cannot help feeling that the adrenalin implicit in standing in front of classes is inherent in the job, and if we did not enjoy that form of heat we would get out of the kitchen. And as stress does set in, you'd think that five minutes in the company of the young would be enough to restore the necessary optimism. Unless of course it's the young who occasion the stress in the first place. But in independent schools, where we have small classes of well-motivated youngsters, that surely cannot be the case.

A young journalist from *The Times* rings, all agog with what he clearly thinks is an exclusive, namely that Boris Yeltsin has left, 'so you won't be allowing armed guards in your classrooms any more.' He does sound abashed when I say that he left on standard transfer two months ago, and that we had never had any armed guards in classrooms in any case. I felt rather sorry for the poor chap and half wished I could have invented for him some really salacious scandal to reward him for his effort. But he and his ilk are so good at doing that anyway that they surely don't need any help from me.

> You cannot hope to bribe or twist
> thank God! The British journalist.
> But, seeing what the man will do
> unbribed, there's no occasion to

Remembrance Day, and the chaplain speaks movingly about people in conflict, illustrating his theme with his collection of British and German medals. I sit next to Chloe from Germany who appreciates our international approach, even though we did sing Jerusalem. But I am most taken by the 2-year-old son of Sian, one of our housemothers. He behaves beautifully throughout the service, thoughtfully and silently aiming his toy gun at all of us in turn. Conflict does not seem to hold too many horrors for him.

This Saturday night, it's the Headmaster's Party, an annual event to which some 200 Upper Sixth pupils and some 25 colleagues and their partners are invited. It is always one of my favourite occasions and people seem to enter very fully into the spirit of the thing, once they realize that the point of it is to meet people whom they may not have met before and to chat to them over drinks and a sumptuous buffet supper. I am conscious almost for the first time that many of our pupils seem more confident and poised than some of our younger staff, who perhaps benefit most from the relaxed occasion. Helen Zhang thanks me for the duck, 'the best I have had since leaving Beijing.' The two Annas, who had told me that afternoon on their way to hockey that they hoped to score three goals each, assured me that in the event they had each scored four.

Matt Perry, who left two years ago, has been chosen to play full back for England against Australia on Saturday. I am reminded that he did not make our 1st XV until his last year. We are delighted for him. Cathy Strongman tells me she is sitting on the chair he used to occupy in her Maths class and is thinking of putting a plaque on it in his honour.

Reading applications for the post of head of our pre-prep school, I was fascinated to come across this example of PC prose from a current headteacher:

I am a committed educationalist with child-centred objectives, capable of developing excellence throughout a school. I have proven ability to organize human and material resources. I enriched my last school, saw the potential for learning and created an atmosphere which was intellectually and visually challenging. I can develop and influence strategic thinking, anticipating constraints and outcomes while reconciling day-to-day demands with longer term objectives.

My God! At least we didn't appoint her, but the fact that one school, apparently undeterred by such robotic garbage, did, reduces my faith in the future of the human race. Or have I got it all wrong? Should I be judging my own role against such criteria, having first taken the trouble to understand what on earth they mean? Perhaps it's just that I am now six months from retirement and the arteries are beginning to harden.

But then next day, in break, I took the senior prefects to hear Nomfundo Walaza from Cape Town, the first black psychologist there, now working with Victims of Violence and Torture. I marvel that anyone, exposed on a daily basis to such profound and widespread pain and anguish in those with whom she works, can remain so obviously balanced, forgiving and tolerant. It is a thoroughly humbling experience to meet her, and faith is at least partly restored.

One poor girl, who is missing her boyfriend at home, has tried incising her wrists—a desperate throw. Later, after the shock of discovery had worn off, she was sitting recuperating with her houseparent who asked her why she thought she had stopped. 'Because it was beginning to hurt,' she replied.

Mrs Aziz flies in from the Yemen—jeans and a leather jacket— to try to sort out her son, who wants to be living it up in London with his friend, and who has been trying to work his passage there with consistently poor behaviour here. She's great.

'I love my son, but he's a manipulative boy and I'm here to win this battle. If I give way now, he'll walk all over me.'

So she's bringing in the Marines in the shape of a 45-year-old British teacher to be his guardian, living in the home they have bought in Street. She's cracked it. If only every parent, blessed—or cursed—with great wealth were as resolute! (Unfortunately, within a very short time, Wa'id does another bunk and we have to admit defeat.)

I dropped in on Tim Nightingale's A-Level English class today. They were reading Carol Ann Duffy's poetry, though this was, admittedly, not immediately obvious as I entered the room. To everyone's delight, the words that greeted me from Tim's reading were 'Fuck off, he said.'

Not surprisingly, parents tend to fire their offspring's bullets because they have no other ammunition to fire. As often as not, they then miss the mark, as happened twice today. One quiet, supportive father, whom I know well, gently remonstrated with me that he had not been informed when his son was interviewed during the course of a cannabis investigation two years ago. We checked with the son and his houseparent and he had never been interviewed at all. The other, an abrasive Scot, gave two tutors a hard time because we had not supplied his daughter with a lockable space. He demanded immediate action etc. Otherwise Heads would roll. Checks revealed that his daughter had always had a lockable locker and this information was conveyed to the father. Was there an apology? Dream on! But then he is estranged from his wife, lives away from the family home and is probably just trying to exercise some paternal testosterone from a distance.

A teacher's private life is seldom, if ever, the business of the Head, unless he or she lives in school accommodation with pastoral responsibility for pupils. In this case, a single, talented but impressionable boarding housemistress has entertained a man

[121]

overnight in her flat on site, and I am therefore constrained to seek an assurance from her that this will not happen again. Indeed, I question her judgement for thinking that it might have been in order in the first place. Things are complicated somewhat in this case though by the fact that the man in question is a hippy, sporting rings appended to various bits of him above and—it is rumoured—below the neck. Would I have taken the same line if he had worn a three piece suit, she asks me. Certainly. In either case the perception among the girls that he is around overnight can only be dispelled if he becomes invisible.

A tour of Georgian Cottage last night. Boys from Indonesia, the USA, Hanoi, Korea, Siberia, Brunei, Turkey, Russia, India and China. The new annexe is proving a real asset. It is spacious, and greatly eases congestion elsewhere in the House. The boys talk of plans, Higher Education, holidays, their homes, sport and their work. Carl Myerscough, the World Junior shot put champion, is thinking of staying on here.

'The facilities aren't matched by any British University,' he says.

UCLA have offered him a very big scholarship, but he also wants to study ceramics.

'Even though the campus is ten miles across, there's no art department there that does ceramics. I'd be better off staying here.'

I am invited to go to Bristol to see *Fidelio* with an Upper Sixth English set. Leila, Sam, Vicky, Neema and Neil sing all the way there in the minibus and all the way back, and are every bit as entertaining as the opera itself. They are also more convincing physically as lively young students than was Fidelio's husband in the opera who, though starving in his prison, was in practice as healthily round as a barrel.

Her Head of Year has gated Polina Yumasheva for various minor infringements. Subsequently I receive a phone call from the Kremlin, asking politely but persuasively if I will waive this punishment temporarily to allow Polina to see Tatyana Yeltsin during her visit to London over the weekend. Having just read of Mr Yeltsin's influence with Saddam Hussein, I am tempted to contrast Iraqi and Millfield approaches to the implementation of our respective rules, but refrain. My refusal to comply is taken with good grace, for which I am grateful.

From out of the blue, we have suffered some gratuitous vandalism in the theatre. Entry has been forced and the phones put out of order. There are no clues until suddenly we have a lucky break. An unguarded remark overheard before a lesson by a prefect, and some investigations with three boys, lead to an admission by Charles T., who had earlier done £300 worth of damage in the Fine Arts Centre, that he was the culprit. He is unable to shed any light on why he should feel constrained to act like this, and I have to say goodbye to him. His poor mother, living offshore, is distraught.

Professor David Crystal talks to the sixth-form about the origins of language and generates huge interest and applause.

'Me Tarzan—you Jane. Was it ever like that?'

'No' is the answer, and he illustrates linguistic subtlety in a number of ways, including fifteen ways of saying 'Yes' by using your voice.

At six months, it transpires, babies gurgle identically in Paris, in Beijing and in London, but by nine months this is no longer the case, as rhythm starts to kick in. *Tum-te-tum* here, but *rat-a-tat* in Paris.

Alexei's father delays his return to Moscow's TV headquarters to bring his wayward son Alexei back after his suspension for harassing others. He shows deeper solidarity with us in our attempts to correct his son's unacceptable conduct than almost any parent I have encountered, and I am impressed. But he does spend three quarters of an hour telling me why he thinks this is important.

Will Scott and Dan Staniforth in the Lower Sixth come to see me with what is a totally new idea. They want to introduce as a Friday afternoon activity Octopush, and have produced a beautifully presented, thoroughly researched and costed proposal to support their request. This sounds at first like a James Bond film but turns out to be underwater hockey. They convince me with ease that they have teams ready to start, rules which make sense (above water at least) and that all is ready to go. So Octopush is launched. Perhaps it has a future on a wider stage, and indeed they subsequently arranged an away fixture with Taunton. If synchronized swimming, where they spend over half their time under water, works in the Olympics, why not Octopush? And with global warming and rising sea-levels, it might have a more immediate impact than even Will thinks.

The school governors met for six and a half hours today, and approved plans to spend £17 million on developments here and at the preparatory school over the next five years. There cannot be many such meetings taking place with such confidence in British schools in the present climate, if indeed there are any. On top of this, the inspection report is to be made available to all parents in full; 10,000 copies will be published. And the strategic plan is approved with only minor amendments. The Executive certainly feels very well supported today.

Tony Blair has exempted Bernie Ecclestone's Formula One show from his ban on tobacco advertising in sport, and my hope that we may see a transformation in British politics is dashed. Nevertheless, I am half tempted to ask Mr Ecclestone to sponsor our new vehicle— a smart golf buggy—which will take prospective parents on their guided tours of the campus. But then again, advertising Benson and Hedges in a smoke-free campus might be seen as provocative. Perhaps we should ask him to sponsor instead the dining hall loos, where the committed smokers currently congregate.

This evening it was the regional round of the English Schools' team swimming championships. We won all twelve races, most of them very easily. At first I began to feel guilty; the others must hate us. But then I remembered the immense dedication of our people, down in the pool at 6 most mornings, and at lunchtime, and again for the evening sessions and I finish by just basking, as usual, in their reflected glory. It is magnificent swimming—a joy to watch, as even our competitors graciously concede.

After a week which includes the HMC Committee held in the National Gallery, where the Holbein and Hogarth exhibition is being held, and a visit to the Queen's Galleries in Buckingham Palace, guided by the keeper of the paintings, I thought I had reached an aesthetic plateau. But then in a single day I had three exemplary letters of extreme clarity, beautifully expressed, from three pupils, and my gratification reached new heights. Daisy Lilley—is this the most fetching name currently at Millfield?—wrote to thank me for a book on the English language; Allie Lindsay wrote to explain in detail her comprehensive plans for a Millfield Eco-action group, and Erica Leeson wrote to tell me of her realistic but meltingly sensitive reactions to a conference on homelessness that she had attended in Bath.

Mrs T. returns from an equestrian event with her daughter and her horse at 10.30 p.m. The poor groom, who had been instructed to await her arrival, not knowing when to expect them, had fallen asleep in the tack room. Mrs. T. loses her temper when she finds the yard closed and shouts abuse at the groom who, though technically off duty at this late hour, nevertheless does everything that is necessary for the horse. Her daughter later apologizes for her mother. Should I remonstrate formally with the wretched woman and risk yet further embarrassment for the daughter? I decide not, but maddeningly find myself awake early the next morning composing the sort of letter I should like to write were it not for the fact that it would only heighten the aggravation all round. But then again...

Showing Bishops Peter and Michael Ball round the school, we came across Louis in the library. He comes from Venezuela and is reading a copy of one of the national papers there, on the Internet, even before it is available on the news stands in Caracas.

Suddenly the press is on to us again and that familiar feeling of being under siege reasserts itself. This time it's something over which we really have no control. It turns out that Prince Charles has bought a copy of the *Big Issue* from a homeless man who tells him that he had been at Millfield. Apparently the *London Standard* has splashed it everywhere. St. James's Palace rings. Is it true that he was here? Records are consulted and yes, Clive Stutter was indeed in the school for two years until 1964. They also want his last known home address. Amazingly, it's St. James's Square.

Tartuffe last night in the theatre. Four hundred people, and three other full houses later in the week. Neema is Dorine, and not only has she just heard that she has won a place at LAMDA for next year, but Sir Tony Jay, he of 'Yes, Prime Minister' fame, whom I took with our party, writes to her to say that she is the best non-professional actor he has seen. You cannot ask for a much more glowing accolade than that.

Paul Howe leaves for the world of work, as others put it. He has been our Chief Swimming Coach for only four years, but has seen us into the 50-metre pool, doubled the size of the elite squad to sixty, and produced strings of internationals even in this short time. And he's only twenty-nine. Our swimmers would kill for him and have just won their second major regional team event in a week for him. This time it was the Open Nationals, so we will be the only school in the finals, alongside all the big UK clubs. Thank heaven, the squad ignored the stewards' announcement urging restraint at the conclusion of the meet, and threw him into the pool. No one was ever chucked in a pool with more affection.

Ben has an aunt, Camilla Carr, who has been taken hostage in Chechnya. This week there is a service to remember her in St. James's Piccadilly, attended by representatives from the FCO and the government, and followed by a press conference. Ben's mother asks me if I can try to contact Tatyana Yeltsin to ask her assistance in obtaining her sister's release. I call Vladimir Vorokov, her UK minder, who immediately offers to help. This very weekend, by an amazing coincidence, he is seeing Mr Rifkin, the Russian politician who is in charge of links with the Chechen government, and promises to take things forward with him. Boris was in the same House as Ben—another amazing coincidence. His aunt is released shortly afterwards though whether there is any link here I have no idea.

I have a card from Jo Beadsworth, a born communicator though not a particularly gifted linguist, who used to be in my German set a couple of years ago.

> Dear Sir,
>
> You always said that if my German class was dropped into Germany by parachute, I'd be the one who would survive the longest. Well now I feel I have been dropped into Hungary, though my Hungarian is much worse than my German. The fencing here is much tougher than in the UK but I hope to surprise them before I leave.
>
> Lots of love from Jo.
>
> P.S. I hope you can use this much paprika.

She was always a spicy girl, so I was not entirely surprised that she had enclosed enough paprika to last me a lifetime. She came to see me a few months later and I learnt that she had gone out to Hungary on spec, with no relevant language skills, job or contacts, had made sufficient money as a waitress to take language and fencing lessons, and had fought well enough to represent GB in the USA. I was so impressed that I made her the subject of one of my school assemblies in the hope that people would get inspired by so much initiative and energy. I'll never know, of course, if they did or not. Such is the fate of most school assemblies, I suspect.

Today sees an entirely novel attempt at pupil fraud. Jon-Pil from Korea makes an appointment to see me. He tells me very politely that he has to leave this term and would I kindly arrange for him to receive his deposit in cash please. The news of his departure comes as a complete surprise so I tell him that I will need confirmation from his father before we can do anything else. Jon-Pil's face falls. Renewed attempts to persuade me of the veracity of his position fall on stony ground and he eventually leaves with a very long face indeed. Enquiries reveal immediately that his father has no knowledge of any proposed departure, and indeed that he would resist any such move with every breath in his body. Suspicions having been aroused here: we make further enquiries and discover that he has incurred massive debts from other pupils, and these are being called in. He is entirely unabashed when I put this to him. 'I just had to try, Sir.'

There is a quad from a houseparent, painting an intriguing picture of a new parent. 'Have you ever met Cristina Carneiro de Mendoza Eastwood? If not, you ought to. She is a law unto herself, mother of Giovanna, a wild Latin, five times married, a lovely lady but one who causes chaos everywhere. Faced with her, I feel I am trying to block a bursting dam with my little finger. I enclose an illegible letter which I think is requesting an early departure at the end of term.'

Today a letter from a current parent, whom I have met, starts 'Dear Sir or Madam'. This is bad enough. Have I really been so long at this job that I have become unsexed? But it gets worse. The signature is incomprehensible so I don't know if this is a man or a woman writing, much as s/he apparently can't tell this of me. The substance of the letter is a bitter complaint about an 'illiterate' circular concerning arrangements for the Duke of Edinburgh's Award next term. I studied the circular carefully and could only see one typo and a misplaced comma. Our correspondent failed completely to acknowledge, let alone express gratitude to, the tutor in charge of D. of E. who is willing to put in countless hours at weekends accompanying the expeditions listed in the original circular. I enjoyed composing my reply!

An agonising interview with an understandably distressed father. While his son gives no evidence here of unhappiness and appears well integrated and positive in all he does, he tells his father that he is being bullied by others in his room. The stories relayed to us sound entirely convincing, and yet are hard to reconcile with the young chap we see in our midst. Father intends to withdraw him immediately. If the stories are true—and we must investigate them now—then this will be the first time that the wrong person has had to leave in a case of bullying. We have work to do.

The last day of term. Some pupils have succeeded in erecting an impressive Millfield sculpture comprising benches and outdoor tables piled twenty-feet high. Even if one could draw a veil over that, on the grounds that there was no damage done, the fact that a bunch of fourth-year boys then start jeering at the stewards who, at some personal risk to themselves, have the dodgy job of deconstructing the sculpture, is really obnoxious. We will have to keep a sharper eye open during the last night of term in future.

But worse is to come. The *Daily Mail* has published today a full page article vilifying the school. No one had taken the trouble to check any of the information with us in advance, so it turns out to be a tissue of fanciful innuendo and invention based on the ageing imagination of someone claiming to have been here as a pupil. In this capacity he suggests he has the up-to-date, inside story on the school. We delve into the records and find that he was indeed here. In fact, he had spent an entire term at Millfield in 1977. He has located five assorted 'scoundrels' who had been at Millfield over the last twenty-five years. They included the *Big Issue* chap, Princess Diana's military lover, a lay clerk at Wells Cathedral about whom some salacious story had appeared in the news recently, and the formidable 'Madam Millfield', whoever she may have been. Apparently she runs a high class brothel in California. We know nothing of her, though she sounds much the most interesting of the bunch.

I talk about the issues raised by such a publication in my four assemblies during the day and find the pupils as outraged by it as I am. In between times, with Abel Hadden, who used to be in my football team at Westminster and who now runs an impressive public relations firm in London, we manage to track down the managing director of the *Daily Mail* on a snow slope at Verbier on a mobile phone. Hopefully, he is embarrassed by the news of this latest example of his impoverished journalism, but I would not bet on it. Serve him right for taking a mobile phone onto the slopes.

The Carol Service in Wells Cathedral makes up for these irritants, and the Britten Ceremony of Carols is really memorable. Afterwards, Adrian White, father of five pupils here and an enterprising governor, muses aloud about making our 400 metre running track into an indoor arena. Has this ever been done before? I wonder naively.

'No. That's what makes it such an exciting project.' He wants to talk more about it next term.

Back in the summer, Sir Robin Buchanan, as Chairman of Governors, had asked me to get my portrait painted; flattering but potentially time consuming. So Julia and I visited the BP exhibition of young portrait painters at the National Portrait Gallery. We followed up four and finally settled on Paul Gildea. Thus the day after Boxing Day I found myself perched on a box in his studio in Brixton, while he did the whole thing in six hours in alla prima style. It's arresting, that's for sure, and is quite unlike any conventional portrait. I think this fits Millfield's adventurous spirit—not a gown, mortar board or leather bound, cliché ridden book in sight. Indeed, even the top part of my head is not in sight, which may make looking at it less painful for people in future. I hope the governors will approve of it, or some of them anyway. Certainly the energy Paul invested in that sustained marathon is evident in the picture, and his manual dexterity is impressive in itself; from paint mixing to thinner, to canvas, wipe brush, change brush, measure, canvas, mix, wipe, thin and so on. And talking all the time.

Chapter 8

The headmaster dons a tutu

JANUARY 1998. At a meeting at Rosemary Brown's house to raise money for master classes for very able youngsters, I met the director of the National Association of Gifted Children. He told me of a 3-year-old girl who learnt to read upside down. She was discouraged, for some reason, from sitting next to her mother as she taught her older brother to read, so she sat opposite them. This on the day when the government turns at least some aspects of education upside down when it announces that it wants private companies to run schools in Education Action Zones.

John Abbot, Director of the 21st Century Learning Initiative working out of Washington, comes before the term starts to give the staff an injection of radical thought on the future of education. Schools, he predicts, will be unrecognizable. The emphasis will be turned around from teaching to pupil learning. Primary teachers will be recruited in larger numbers, class sizes in primary schools will shrink, and pupils will be given their Heads to learn what really interests them, almost regardless of what that is. But *really* learn! At the time when their learning antennae are at their most acute, children will be encouraged to enjoy researching their main areas of interest in depth. It all seems to tie up with the little girl who reads upside down.

We need to exploit our independence in schools in what is becoming an increasingly controlled, centralized educational environment.

A quad from Giles Neeve. 'There is a bald girl in the school—Angelica. She has had her head shaved in the holidays. The Senior Mistress, with the wisdom of Athene, has declared that she shall wear a hat for a fortnight until such time as the absence of hair can be re-assessed, thus confirming the old adage, ' "If you want to wear a hat, shave your head".'

Day One, and as always I am as nervous as a kitten at the start of term. Four assemblies to the various year groups really take it out of me, and no doubt out of my long suffering audiences as well. I quote at one point George Bernard Shaw, 'The only time my education was interrupted was when I was in school.'

Afterwards, I hear one Lower Sixth boy, talking to a pal as he left, say, '*Now* he tells us.'

Day Two. Parents for most of the day. Mrs Khanchandani, worried that the financial melt down on the Pacific Rim may mean she will not be able to return Jiten as she would have wanted. We'll work something out. Then Ian Woosnam with his wife and Daniel, who said he'd like to join the school today.

'So would I,' says his father.

They leave early to fly back by helicopter to Guernsey before the next bad weather front moves in. Then Mr Thaung from Burma, who presses us to be his guests there and even talks of setting up a British school there with me as consultant. A generous, spontaneous and deeply unconsidered thought. Next comes the Marquess of Kildare with Polyanna. She is mad keen on hockey and is wonderfully communicative—a natural for Millfield. Then Mr and Mrs M., who are worried that their daughter has not settled down too well and are consequently debating a change of House or even of school. They are clear sighted, supportive people with an unhappy daughter. I am sure things will work out all right, given enough time. But of course, as usual, what is 'enough'?

Shirley Harrison brings back her young hockey players from the regional school finals, where they apparently played their socks off to lose eventually in the final, 2–1 on penalty strokes, to last year's champions. They were naturally disappointed by the result, but happily remorse faded when they were faced with a Big Mac each on the motorway coming back.

Pascale Rouprich took the ski trip again this year. The pupils, of all ages and all levels of experience, conducted themselves in an exemplary way and were appreciative company; clearly a very successful trip. But at Heathrow, on their return, only one parent bothered even to acknowledge her presence, let alone thank her for arranging and leading the entire thing so well. It confirms my view that it's the adult generation that needs schooling more than the young.

Angelika, our bald anarchist, tells us she is depressed. We offer help. No, she insists, she does not want to be cured of her depression. How can you be a good anarchist if you're at peace with yourself? Catch 22. She goes further—literally—by slipping out of her House at night and going for a walk up the Tor. The walks, she says, are an essential part of her anarchy. Her delightful mother comes over from Greece to discuss the matter with us. Her parents are respectively professors of Greek and English literature at the University in Athens. We agree that we need to find a formula that will fall just short of requiring Angelika to compromise her principles while allowing me legitimately to keep her in the school. This is the same week when the two pigs destined for the slaughter-house—the Tamworth Two— did a bunk to the abattoir, swam a river and high-hoofed it to open countryside. A popular rumour went that the airports had been alerted in case they tried to slip aboard a plane to seek sanctuary in Israel. Angelika would certainly sympathize with their motives.

I am flattered to read the text of a speech by a Ugandan headmaster at a school with which I established an exchange programme with Bristol Cathedral School years ago. He refers to me as 'the much revered headmaster.' Perhaps it is just as well that my immediate family greets this with howls of derisive laughter.

One poor girl has broken her jaw and has been told by her doctor not to speak for a fortnight. Her group tutor sends round a note to her teachers, pointing out that since she is a quiet girl at the best of times, this may not make much difference to her classroom performance at all.

Three mornings running at around 7.30, Tatiphon, a shy Thai girl who has just won a conditional place to Cambridge, comes to see me before breakfast to discuss her fees in the light of the massive devaluation of the Thai bhat. Each time she gives me a start as I look up from my desk to find that she has made a silent entrance and is standing patiently by my side waiting for me to see her. She can't weigh more than five stone, I should think, but since she has a black belt in Karate, I don't feel inclined to remonstrate. The fee issue is not an easy one, for it affects quite a few of our people on the Pacific Rim, but we must of course work something out soon.

In a glacial wind and driving rain, our 3rd Hockey XI are playing Downside. Their reserve tells me the score when I ask and adds, through chattering teeth, that he thinks our umpire is biased against them. Later, a parent who is himself a qualified hockey umpire, expresses admiration for the quality of the umpiring on such a fast surface and in such conditions. Looking for scapegoats for our shortcomings is, I suppose, a trait we all have in common to some extent. Later that afternoon, three consecutive sets of parents would seem to exemplify this. Each pair was separated, and each had come together at, I assume, great personal and emotional cost, to discuss their concerns about their children. No matter how hard they tried to conduct themselves in a civilized way, in each case there were undertones of mutual blame. It was truly distressing to see good people in such a pickle. I felt utterly drained at the end of it all.

The inspection report has been published to all parents with a preface by the Chairman of Governors. I wait for parental reactions. First out of the blocks to the Chairman is the Judge, who fires off a broadside of complaint about almost every aspect of the school. I would have been disappointed if he hadn't for it would have been out of character. At least he's being true to form. Another parent, himself a school owner, recognizes it as being a flattering report of which we should be proud. Perhaps people are taken aback by the restrained inspector-speak, for inspectors are not allowed to use emotive or extravagant language. On the first page, for example, Millfield is described as 'a good school.' When I first saw this in draft form, knowing how excited the inspection team had been by almost everything they had seen here, I rang the team leader to query his adjective. What's wrong with adjectives such as outstanding, superb or even electrifying? I was told that 'good' meant good, and that, had we been even slightly less than good, the sentence would have read, 'Millfield is a good school with room for improvement in some areas.'

The best reaction came at the end of the week from a father who had picked up on this linguistic style.

'It sort of misses the point,' 'he said. 'It's rather like Queen Victoria watching Arsenal.'

The chaplain has a spiritual and a liturgical problem on his hands for he has been asked by the stable staff to come and exorcize the stables. Something is wrong in the equine world. It's not as heavy as a poltergeist, more some sort of aura apparently. Are the horses themselves affected by this, one wonders, or are they indeed the cause of the general alarm? Have too many people been reading *Equus*? Anyway, Simon sallies forth to do his stuff.

Colonel H. sends another long letter, the sort that used to be written on asbestos paper when that was allowed. It is now eight months since his daughter left, since when he has failed to answer any of my various letters. Now he accuses us of a number of sins of omission, and ends with the cheap jibe that he has seen that article in the *Daily Mail* and perhaps there is some truth in the conspiracy theory after all?

By happy coincidence, the next thing that surfaces in the in-tray is a copy of a third-former's essay, sent to me by his thoughtful English tutor to cheer me up, in which he rebuts all the arguments in the *Mail* article. It ends: 'The thing I like most about our school is the atmosphere of good humour and friendship. I certainly would not want to be anywhere else.' But the thing I like best about that piece is his reference to *our* school.

A *News of the World* reporter calls, claiming to have been told that we are starting random drug testing. I tell him that there is no truth in his assertion. I explain our policy, now several years old, whereby we test only those whose conduct gives us cause to suspect that they may have been taking illegal drugs. This does not stop him from writing a twenty-line piece, stating that 'Millfield has begun spot drug tests.' There are five other inaccurate statements as well. I should have recorded the conversation of course, but experience is what you get five minutes after you needed it. What should I do? Ask them to print a retraction? Fat chance. Or try the Press Complaints procedure? This would risk a slanging match and recriminatory articles to follow, and Marlborough's experience years ago shows what can happen when the press really have it in for you. So discretion is the better part of valour, again. And anyway, which of our parents is likely to read the *News of the World*? It is no surprise to see the Henley Centre's survey this week showing that only 7% of us trust the press.

A fire engine appears outside the stables. It transpires that a horse has fallen in the horse-walking machine and got trapped. Luckily it survives the experience and is pulled out. It was precisely the same horse that had jumped over the hedge in the summer into the Somerton road. It seems that it is always in trouble. Is this suspension or expulsion?

There is a lively discussion following a sixth-form lecture on HIV/AIDS, but at one point our lecturer gets the sort of answer you don't normally plan for. He was challenging the pupils to identify with the fringe issues.

'You go for a job and someone with AIDS gets it instead of you. What do you think?'

To which one of our less sensitive souls replies, 'I think I'll get the job when he dies.'

I take Stephanie Owen, Young Musician of the Year semi-finalist, Isla McRae, harpist, Kirsten Griffiths and Ali Oyston, violinists, to The Rib, Hilly and Michael Cansdale's house next to Wells Cathedral, to perform in their mediaeval hall in aid of Save the Children. They look dazzling in their evening dresses, play breathtakingly well and then charm the socks off everyone afterwards. I am quite unreasonably proud of them, having played no part in their triumph other than as their chauffeur. But I am aware that none of them has been practising for less than ten years. That is why they are so stunningly accomplished. That plus raw talent.

Jo Edwards, a good marathon runner and even better mathematician, and I are watching Barney Stephenson win the Mendip Open cross-country with characteristic grit. She remarks how foolish the Cambridge dons were to have missed him this year. I observe absent-mindedly that they missed me too, to which Jo replies with conviction, 'That's more understandable.'

I have appointed this week three good couples as houseparents to the three boarding houses which become available in September, but only after weeks of working at it, and with no spares left at the moment if other houses unexpectedly fall vacant. Will the future here hold the prospect of non-residential houseparents, as is already the practice in some schools elsewhere? Things are becoming more complicated as teachers become more selective about the type of house within which they would be willing to serve, e.g. boys, girls, big, small, in-house, out-house etc. It is the key pastoral role in the school, as often as not the determining factor in a youngster's development and happiness while at Millfield, so getting these things right is one of the most important things I do. But with twenty-eight boarding houses it's not a matter that is ever completely out of my mind.

A head-count of those parents who are on the brink of litigation against me reveals: Col. H., who withdrew his daughter nine months ago having vented his spleen on tutors throughout her time here; Mr S., who never complained of anything while his son was here, even when pressed to do so by me, but who withdrew him without warning or consultation after a term and now threatens action against fees in lieu of notice; Mr L., who wants his son to have the lead part for the second year running in his year group's play, and who—astonishingly—will not accept that others should have their turn; and Mr W., whose son was unable to see himself other than as the centre of the universe and who made no effort to fit in during his short time here. All are inspired by money. Three are single fathers, and I imagine need to try to impress their offspring that they are fighting on their behalf, though how their current actions can be of benefit to their children, I cannot imagine.

We advertised last week on the same day for a PE teacher and a Physicist. Within twenty-four hours, we had 198 enquiries for the first and 25 for the second. This would seem to confirm the news this week that now only PE and two arts subjects are *not* considered to be teacher shortage subjects. Eventually, from over 200 applications for the PE post, I appointed the current captain of the Welsh Hockey team.

It is Art Scholarship week and Len Green, our most imaginative and enterprising Director of Art, and the highly qualified but less experienced Head of Art in the preparatory school cannot agree on those to whom they should be offered. Naturally I back Len, but some sort of rapprochement between them must be developed if the spectre of the preparatory school's best artists heading elsewhere is not to become reality. Already there is an indication of this, for the top art scholar to Marlborough this year does not even feature on Len's list of possible candidates.

We have amended the houseparents' contract for housemothers who work outside the school. From September their allowance will shrink by the amount they earn elsewhere. I have passed these details to everyone who has expressed interest in next year's posts—except, by a dreadful oversight—the one couple most affected and whom I most want to accept the house we have discussed at some length already. It's my cock-up, and they accept my apology with good humour and make it easy for me.

Today it's the Gang of Four—the lunch we have every term here with the headmasters of Clifton, Bryanston and Marlborough, all of whom run large boarding schools and who instinctively understand the thrills and spills of the trade. There is never any agenda, just gales of laughter and the chance to be entirely undiplomatic for a change. I think we have no professional secrets from each other, and just greatly enjoy each other's company. It is very therapeutic.

Christa, our Romanian scholar this year, has been paying £200 a term towards the cost of her food. In the same post as a request from her mother that her food be provided free of cost comes a letter from HRH Prince Paul of Romania, who wants to contact the Class of '68, with whom he was here as a boy. His timing could hardly be better and I have put him in touch with Christa's mother in the hope that he may be willing to sponsor Christa.

A small group of boys come to see me in great distress. One of their good friends who left last year finds himself in an almost impossible position. His mother had killed herself earlier, but now his father has taken his own life too. It is hard to know what on earth to do at this remove for the best, other than to arrange support for his friends.

I have to ring poor Iris S. to tell her that we can no longer hang on to her son. He is a pleasant enough chap, but simply cannot get up in the morning. When he does, he is so laid back in class that he confuses others. She is the best of women, but we have all tried in vain to motivate him and he now seems to need additional expert help. We talk at length, but eventually I have to leave her in order to visit Joyce Meyer, the widow of our Founder Jack Meyer, on what turns out to be her last night based in Somerset since she settled here on her return from India in 1935. She has deteriorated significantly in the last two weeks and her daughter has now arranged for her to be looked after closer to her home in Surrey. I give her John Rae's most recent book, *Letters to Parents: How to Get the Best Available Education for Your Child*, in which Jack is featured, and read her some extracts from it, but I think it is all a bit too much for her. It is a very moving parting and to my great regret turns out to be the last time I see her alive.

The staff in the medical centre were subjected to a real ordeal last night. Our bald anarchist had bought some beer, got drunk and attacked one of our nurses. Worse, she had also given some of it to Jodie, who still suffers from a severe eating disorder and is thus incapable of absorbing alcohol. She had to be ambulanced to Taunton. The future of both of them here looks bleak indeed, for Jodie cannot cope with boarding, having previously failed to cope as a day girl. Angelika has within the last couple of days terrified the third-year girls in her House by showing them a length of rope 'for hanging herself with.' She will not be able to board here any longer.

Half-term starts today, and the pressure gauge of things that have to be done before everyone leaves is high. Breakfast at 7.30 with the first people in, always the girls from Warner House. At 8.30, the fifth-form assembly, given by the sixth-form, a pastiche of life at the top end of the school, aimed at encouraging those who may be contemplating leaving into staying for what is, we all agree, the best bit of the school, namely the sixth-form. Then a series of interviews for our IT post, but no suitable candidate presents himself so we hastily arrange for other candidates to come in this afternoon. My General Studies lesson comes as a welcome break from everything else—some might say a self-indulgent escape from more pressing duties, but these lessons are almost the only moments in the week when I am not disturbed. This is followed by the soap box announcements in the staff common room and a cabinet meeting to discuss monitoring attendance at lunch, given the fact that some of our eating-disordered girls are avoiding it so as to eat less, while others are choosing to eat in Street at the Chinese restaurant, possibly so as to eat more. One can sympathize with those overseas pupils for whom English food is too bland, but there is such a wide choice nowadays, with no constraint on how much you eat, that the cost to parents of paying twice for lunch cannot be justified, so our battle with pupils, and with the Chinese restaurant, continues. Not surprisingly, we get no co-operation from the owner, who allows pupils in at the back if we have prefects stationed at the front. It is tempting to turn a blind eye in this case, given that it's looking like a battle we cannot win, but perhaps strengthening the prefect team responsible for Street may yet carry the day.

Suniti then comes to measure me for my tutu, for the part of the fairy godmother in the staff pantomime, which the pupils are producing. Any stranger coming into my office at that moment would have called social services to complain of headmaster abuse. Phil Cooper came to lunch and then did his splendid presentation on drugs to the sixth-form. He is a recovered heroin addict and has many impressive scars to prove it. He also writes arresting poetry. Coming from someone who knows from experience what drugs can do to you, his warnings have far more effect than if they'd come from the likes of me, with no experience. He always mentions that I was the first Head to offer him a platform, which is kind of him, and now he's working in schools from Gordonstoun to Wellington.

More IT interviews, with more success this time, Katayun Engineer collecting her son for the holiday, and two houseparents to talk about tricky relationships in their House. The most intriguing part of all this is the oral report from the lecturer at the Manchester College of Music, who has been conducting a three day review of our wind section, and who has some pretty trenchant criticisms to make of our current provision. Has the fact that we have had three nationally rated flautists here for three consecutive years blinded us, or deafened us, to less than inspirational provision elsewhere? A last IT interview with a 45-year-old who looks 25, despite having produced seven children, followed by the appointments meeting, phone calls to the candidates, and thence to the in-tray at 6.30. Finally there is a little party for Jo, our cleaner, who leaves tonight on maternity leave. I get home by 8 to prepare for our departure for Bombay at dawn tomorrow on the next, and for me the last, recruitment tour of India.

Eight days later, we are back in Street from Delhi via Amsterdam at 4 on the Sunday afternoon, leaving me just time to get into the last two hours of the fifth-form Parents' Evening, by the end of which I am running on empty.

Suniti comes for a second fitting of the tutu, but this time, by mutual agreement, to avoid any risk of her being expelled or my getting the sack, she brings a friend as chaperone, for fitting a tutu, as I soon discover, can be a disconcertingly personal business.

A group of South African sportsmen—all white as it turns out—arrive for a 24-hour stay and immediately adopt that furrow-browed, prejudiced approach which I have come to associate with this species. Uninvited, they launch immediately into what they see as corruption in their current cabinet.

'Mandela's daughter was found to be a passenger in a stolen car.'

'But she isn't in the cabinet, is she?'

'No, but it goes to show, doesn't it? All you see nowadays is new money.'

How on earth they thought that *old* money could have been accumulated by black South Africans under the Apartheid regime, heaven alone knows.

A young member of staff comes to see me, awkwardly at first, to tell me that he would like to be an assistant houseparent. This is good news, for he's an admirable man with a naturally encouraging way with the young. But he wants to put me fully in the picture regarding his private life. He tells me he has a 9-month-old son by a woman with whom he no longer lives. Would this make a difference to his wish to serve in a boarding house? I already admire him as a teacher, but do so the more for his willingness to take full responsibility for his son, even in difficult circumstances. His integrity shines through. I have no doubt that he will be a very good role model in a House and will try to appoint him as soon as a vacancy occurs.

I have a letter from Cuong's grandfather in Hanoi, to whom I spoke in French when we were there. His gratitude to the school is generous to the point of extravagance.

'Je crois que le saint Christophe Martin choisit parmi ceux qui ont une bonne étoile pour leur montrer la lumière.'

It will be hard to live up to his expectations of us, that's for sure.

I saw Mr and Mrs B. about their very talented musical son. I had to see them alone because the Director of Music, who would normally join me for such a discussion, had accepted an invitation to adjudicate somewhere in the depths of Wales. They were pleasant people but were clearly addicted worriers. This would explain in part their son's prodigious capacity for over-anxiety. In this case, he had allowed a minor incident involving the Director to fester in his mind for nearly six months and had never thought to talk it over with him. Once the family had ventilated all this, the boil seemed to have been lanced and hopefully the son will now go from strength to strength.

The Chairman of the Common Room comes in with a long face. He is concerned about the core load for teachers, seeing in it increased commitments where I see no more than a rationalisation of existing practice. I suppose this sort of thing is at the heart of most management versus trades union disputes, but I find it dispiriting. He's a good teacher but his glass is too often half empty. It was he who once wrote pointing out that he had slipped on some untreated ice one morning 'and had nearly seriously grazed my shin.'

Leeds United U14 and U16 youth sides come for their annual weekend here, training with us on the Saturday, staying overnight in the Houses with the boys, and playing us on the Sunday morning. It's Phil Cookson's brainwave and a great favourite with both sides. We lost both but they were fine matches and the visiting boys' focused approach to football will have taught our people a great deal.

Sue Woods challenged a third-year boy about where he had been at lunchtime. She was surprised to hear him say candidly, with no trace of irony, 'I've been down in Street, at Gossips coffee shop. Teachers aren't allowed in there.'

Three Cornish representative sides come to play soccer against us. Inadvertently, the stewards only lock one changing room and £150 is stolen from wallets in the other two. It's a wretched business, of course, made worse by the thought that there is a predatory junior somewhere out there hanging about trying doors, waiting his chance.

A girl in the fifth-form complains that two Russian boys in the Upper Sixth have molested her in the weights room, touching her breasts and making suggestive comments. Both the boys are on a last warning for misbehaviour and both face their last exams here in three months time. But the girl, whom I believe, knows the boys well and is indeed quite friendly with them. Could it have been a misunderstanding on her part, as they claim?

'As God is my witness,' says one of them dramatically, 'she is a liar.'

There are interviews with teachers, other pupils, and houseparents. It all takes a lot of time and emotional effort, and in the end the position is still not cut and dried. But then these things seldom are. On the strength of what is known, I cannot justify refusing to allow the boys to see their courses through to their conclusion, but their freedom of movement around the school will have to be carefully controlled when they return from a two week suspension.

Polo players have not always struck me as being aesthetes, but I am revising my view having come across Andrew, in the Lower Sixth, conducting a most civilized practice session in the indoor riding school to the strains of Swan Lake booming out from the public address system.

Cannabis is found behind the bed of a boy in Kingweston House. He tests positive. It is profoundly disappointing, for he is one of only two boys whom I have so far allowed back from suspension, following his admission of a first offence a year ago. He now leaves. Then his room-mates have to be questioned. One is a very pleasant chap who is easily led, easily distracted, finds work hard and struggles to keep up. To my utter dismay, he admits having smoked cannabis last weekend. Had he not shared a room with the original culprit, he'd never have been questioned, and might never have been drawn into smoking in the first place. And of course, if he had lied, we'd never have known of his involvement at all. I am going to allow him back after a two-week suspension. He writes me a long, painful, fairly legible letter, which I find very touching. 'Although I am not very good academically, nor very sporty, I have a good heart.' I agree.

Claire Shimmel and I hold an evening's in-service training session for forty-five houseparents with the title, 'What is pastoral care?' Among other things we conclude that it is 'Being there.' On the way out, Peter Mills, tongue in cheek, asks, 'If being there is what it's all about, how come we are here?'

A look at the calendar reveals that out of twenty-six term-time evenings this month, we are out on school business for twenty of them. No wonder it is proving so hard to fit in rehearsals for the staff pantomime.

A Thai boy is found to have brought pornographic CDs into the UK from his home in Dubai. When accused by his houseparent, he said lamely that he had meant to take them back again but had a cold and couldn't. 'He coughed a few times to reinforce this claim.'

We then learn that this was not at half-term but last weekend when he had an exeat for London but actually took off for Dubai for two days to see his girlfriend, unknown to his parents. This was the chap whose father just last week had offered to pay for a new boarding house here! He is suspended for two weeks—in Dubai, of course, which is just where he wants to be anyway.

I have received a booklet entitled 'UFO Concern'. There is an introductory letter from an unknown author addressed to 'Dear Mr Headmaster', in which he enjoins me 'to read it carefully so that you will then be in a better position to deal appropriately with the UFO problem within your own sphere of influence'. I have heard it said that headmasters wield more power than cabinet ministers but I have never aspired to celestial power on this scale before.

Thirty bursars spend the day in the school for a conference. What is the collective noun for bursars? Many are suggested, some unprintable, but coven seems to win. To my surprise and delight, rather than the prodigious facilities, it is the friendliness and courtesy of the pupils they have met that attracts most of their comment to me as they leave.

A third-form tutor group does an assembly on the theme that I have lifted all bans on smoking, alcohol and drugs. They enjoy drunken classes, have a ball, then start some serious coughing, and finally the 1st XI loses to Butleigh Village 3rd team. At that point they vote to revert to rules. It is snappy, fun, not too heavy on the good sense and very encouraging to see them devising such original stuff so early in their time here.

Nadia Rice, 50 years old, mother of Sam and Gareth, both of whom were here, lectured on her rowing race across the Atlantic with her husband. They came third, ahead of the Royal Marines. She was inspirational, a born teacher and committed minimalist, and I have no doubt that 400 people will not forget the realization that dawned on us all as she spoke that 'ordinary' people, among whom she counted herself, are capable of 'extraordinary' things.

A Libyan boy, with a father who claims to have been close to the pre-Gaddafi Prime Minister, is in trouble. Defiance of staff, disruptive behaviour in class and now pornographic material in school. There are thirteen written complaints in the file about him this term alone. His parents come to see me. His father beats his chest, literally, in dismay and then turns to his wife and shouts angrily, 'I have done my part with this boy. It is your job to raise him. My name, not yours, is dragged through the mud by his conduct. You can pack your bags and take the child. I can do no more.'

His wife, for whom I have quickly developed the utmost sympathy, is clearly distressed by this but puts a heroically brave face on it. Perhaps I am more shaken than she is, for I suspect this is not the first time she has heard this sort of stuff. Calm is eventually restored, and I offer, reluctantly, a further term's probation here—after suspension— mainly on humanitarian grounds, since one option being explored by the father is that his son be interned in a Moslem seminary to become a mullah. 'That would teach him,' he says as he leaves. I have never considered before that training for religious leadership could be inflicted on the young as a punishment for youthful transgressions.

Within twenty-four hours of this conversation, on Sunday morning, I have half an hour on the phone with the father of the boy who supplied the pornography in the first place, and who has also been suspended for a week. He lives in North London and from the outset explains that he has a social position to maintain. He is outraged at my punishment of his son, but seems more concerned about what his neighbours and friends are going to think about it than about the lessons to be learnt for his son.

'My friends are just going to snigger at this,' he snorts, 'It's laughable.'

I say I cannot be responsible for the reactions of his London cronies, but he returns repeatedly to the theme. Could one imagine two more different sets of reactions from any two families one could locate anywhere?

Luke, a 26-year-old horse much loved by all the riders, falls into a full ditch and gets completely stuck. It takes two fire-engine crews to pull him out, and then only after a two hour struggle. I see Luke in the solarium shortly afterwards and he is asleep on his feet. If what one of the riders tells me is true, he is the equivalent of 140 human years old, so no wonder.

A good but concerned family see me about their son, who says he is being victimized by his peers, and wants to leave. He is in a good House, which by chance we visited last week, in a room with three other delightful, well mannered boys, and in class, games, and socially, is making his mark. On the face of it, he is happy and well integrated. Further investigation is inhibited by his wish that the names of those who he claims are getting at him are not to be revealed. It is a poser. We are certain that he will be fine, but things are not helped by the fact that his pals from his last school are all being educated elsewhere, and he calls them up regularly. The phone is not an asset in this case, for it seems clear that his attempts to hang on to the past are inhibiting his ability to make the most of the present.

We have a boy who drinks between four and six pints of water every evening and wets his bed every night. This entails two lots of washing every day. His mother refuses to allow his houseparents, who have taken immense trouble to support the lad, to ask our school doctor to talk to the boy, but gives no reason for her stance. It is an impasse, but having sought and failed to secure parental support for further action, I feel our hands are now tied, at least for a while.

William Louey is here to see his eight Beijing scholars. It seems that the Chinese government is now making objections to the scheme, for they fear the youngsters—some of their finest assets—may not return to China. Consequently, headteachers there are now reluctant to recommend their top students. All very understandable, and indeed there is no guarantee that they will return after Millfield, Oxbridge and an MBA at Harvard, which is the plan. As William puts it, 'Who would want to return to take up jobs like managing a toy factory? The best people will always go where the opportunities are.'

Reports reach me that the boy who supplied the pornography recently has actually had a shot at filming his own. Reeling from this indication of a novel area of pupil deviancy, I go straight into a meeting with governors and our consultants on the plans for our new dining hall, which looks set to cost £3 million. From the salacious to the salivating.

A new 14-year-old has been caught drinking, and this on top of a smoking offence. I took him from another HMC school to give him a second chance. A second chance for what, I now ask myself. He is unrepentant, indeed, aggressive, showing real attitude. I take another close look at his reference. It is supportive, but now I can spot an ambiguous sentence: 'We have recommended Millfield because J. is more likely to prosper on the larger stage with you than in our much smaller school.' When I call the Head to test out this comment, it translates as 'He'd have been fired if he hadn't left. He was in trouble in and out of school. He had a very strong influence on others. I'm not surprised he's giving trouble.' Thanks a lot! Now it's up to me to fire him instead, but at a cost to teachers and pupils here that I much regret.

We spend the evening at St. Anne's House. The atmosphere is transformed by the new houseparents, both of whom relish the company of the boys who are themselves once more able to talk with openness and candour. Neil, in the Upper Sixth, shows us round: one of life's born enthusiasts, who is clearly fond of everyone. He is known universally as Monster and loves it. He shows us his word-sensitive computer. He talks into it and it types up his message on the screen. He lets me have a go, and it comes up with complete rubbish, but then apparently it took six hours before it got to know Neil well enough to make sense of him. One young chap has his biology prep on the brain. What had he learnt in biology today? 'I think I learnt that the big part of my brain is smaller than the small part.'

Sarah Champion tells me that she has had to remonstrate with a Korean boy for fighting.

'But he hit me first, Miss.'

'Well you mustn't hit back.'

'What I do then, Miss? You want I stand there, cry like baby and call Mummy?'

Sarah was inclined to see his point and apparently replied, 'No, perhaps you should just hit him back like you said.'

Mike and Marna Brearley come for the week-end. He lectures to the sixth-form and is brilliant at fielding questions, which rattle around bewilderingly between cricket, leadership and psychology. These seem to come at him almost antiphonally: 'Do you go along with Freud's view on hedonism?' 'What do you think of Atherton as a captain?' 'Is Utilitarianism a sensible code for life?' 'How did you manage to get the best out of Botham?'

In the evening, we take them to this year's 'Expressive Edge', two hours of dance involving our seventy dancers, technicians, sound and light people and a battery of drummers. It is superbly invigorating, slick, packed with energy, well rehearsed, snappy. I've often told Mike, with whom I have sailed quite a lot, that I have the best job in education, and he says he now sees why.

The advertisement for the 'Strawberries and Wine' concert has come out as 'Strawberries and Wind.'

At their assembly this morning, the fifth-formers gave two impressive demonstrations. In one tutor group, the boys had been taught to play the recorder by the girls, and proved it by playing a piece accompanied by their teachers. The girls, meanwhile, had been taught how to manage line-outs and scrums, including the scrum grunt, by the boys. They were properly dressed for action and demonstrated their new skills with enthusiasm against the boys. Their tutor told me afterwards that they had not really bonded very well before this inspired move, but they do now, especially in the scrum.

I have just spent two good days at Sherborne School for Girls as a member of a small group of six, working on scenario planning for independent education. It was most stimulating. At first, I thought it was merely an intellectual exercise, but by the end we were convinced there were messages there for the sector as a whole, and were discussing the routes through which these could best be ventilated. Globalization, the privatization of education nationally, the IT revolution, financial implosion, an ageing population, short term contracts, optimum learning methods and ages, teacher shortages, the changing roles of teachers and redundant exams (GCSE) all featured in our thinking. Along the way, it was fascinating to learn that one in every five meals eaten in this country is eaten in a car, and that Sweden's favourite beer is brewed in Japan.

I got back at the end of the second day in time to see Olivia, who had a bruised face and who had spent last night in a car, having been locked out of her home by her parents. She tells me they have now changed the locks on their doors in an apparent attempt to ensure she cannot return home at all. This is likely to become a case for social services, but right now it's a matter of trying to offer the reassurance she so desperately needs and fix her up for the foreseeable future in a boarding house, as a temporary refuge from home.

Yesterday was the Staff Pantomime, *Cinderella*, directed, produced, lit and staged by the Lower Sixth in a unique reversal of roles which we had all enjoyed in rehearsal immensely. Dan and Mia had done a splendid job of making my colleagues and me learn our lines, turn up punctually and give the whole enterprise what style we could produce. The invisible lines between teachers and pupils were rendered delightfully fuzzy by our drag and their direction. Jenny, my incomparable secretary, with a solution to every problem, lent me her leotard, Suniti produced my tutu, and made me up as a fiendish Fairy Godmother. We did two performances, a matinee and an evening performance, to 800 wildly appreciative pupils and raised £1,600 for African children suffering from AIDS in Nairobi. Between the two shows, I had to rush home and host a dinner for a number of governors to discuss the future constitution of the governing body. I managed to hide the leotard under my suit, but traces of fairy godmother make-up shook my guests visibly as they arrived.

As Sir Robin said in his incomparable fashion afterwards, 'Christopher, this is the sort of thing you can do in your last year, but not in your first.' Too true.

The next day, Julia laid the foundation stone for Martin's House. governors were there, and houseparents and senior staff, and we all had champagne in the sunshine. As her name emerged from behind the little blue curtain erected for the occasion, I was unexpectedly moved. Being a headmaster's wife is such a very tricky business. You can easily do too much and get in the way of the professionals, or not enough and be thought stand-offish. In my view, biased as it is, Julia gets it just right, and I take this moment as recognition from Millfield of all that she has brought to this place these last eight years.

At the governors' meeting that follows, Dick Ransley, whose tongue is never out of his cheek, starts his presentation on General Studies by saying how reassured he is to see the headmaster in a suit for a change, rather than a tutu. Earlier, a young girl had made a point of coming up to let me know that, 'Purple suits you, Sir.'

The worst thing this week has certainly been the culmination of the problems poor Katie has been having. Suspended for drinking, this brilliant, athletic, but now dangerously thin perfectionist has lost another 1.5 kilos and has been vomiting in her House. The effect of all this on her friends is getting serious, and her own health is clearly in jeopardy. I have now had to send her away until September, to return then only if certain very clear conditions involving weight gain have been met. Hugh Sharp, our doctor, has been immensely helpful at every stage of this profoundly depressing business, and our protocol on eating disorders has proved useful too, but the emotional chaos occasioned for family and friends is dreadful to behold.

While we were enjoying the Prefects' Dinner for 120 in the dining hall, with the prefects immaculate in away-match dress and on sparkling form, Holmcroft House, we later discover, has been under siege. A sizeable contingent of local twelve-to-sixteen-year olds, who have been doing some serious drinking, have been provoking retaliation from our boys, who are trying to get on with their prep and are in any case under strict orders not to respond. At one point, however, Chris Coates, the houseparent, has to drive a boy up to the medical centre. (He has broken his nose while rehearsing a fight sequence for next week's House drama competition.) As he opens the gates to drive through, the gang outside sense vulnerability and crowd in. They invade the games room, punch and kick two of our younger boys and are eventually persuaded to leave by diplomatic, and large, seniors. The ringleaders are well known to us. Do we ask the police to prosecute, and risk provoking further, worse attacks? Or play it down in the hope that they will get bored and go elsewhere on Friday nights? I will follow it up with the very helpful youth club leader, outside whose premises the lads get their drink from the back of cars driven round by older people. We will work out a *modus vivendi*, I'm sure.

Triumphalism is another sin, I know, but it is particularly good to hear that Kirsten and Allie, our two star violinists, came first and second in the string section of the Mid-Somerset Festival, beating contestants from Wells Cathedral School, which is one of just a small cluster of specialist music schools in the country.

Huong-Joon, a Korean boy, joined us two years ago with almost no English. Only his determination, a fine sense of humour and the support of his teachers have seen him through, but that's a pretty powerful combination, of course. Yesterday, he suffered a torsion of the testicle and was taken to hospital by Dick Boustead, his housemaster. A woman doctor examined him, to his intense embarrassment.

'Does it always hang like this?' she asked him.

Fixing the ceiling stoically, Huong-Joon apparently replied, 'Don't know. I never watch it.'

Seven of our eight Senior House plays this year are home grown, written by boys and girls with their likely casts in mind. This is the culmination of a trend which has been developing for some years now, and which will, I hope, continue. The themes for most of them, however, are the thin line between sanity and madness, and of course death. What do most of these vigorous young people know of death, anyway? At their age they tend to see themselves as being immune to death. Mortality has no meaning for them, other than purely intellectually. Is it just because it's near the end of term and it's been raining a lot, or should I worry about this, on top of everything else? I'm reminded of Mme de Sévigné, who once said of museums that what she saw tired her and what she did not see worried her.

At breakfast, I came across a group of immaculately dressed boys who turned out to be a visiting hockey side from South Africa. I talked to the captain, whose account of the match yesterday (which we won 9–0) was both enthusiastic and rational. I assumed immediately that he was an inspirational captain, an impression later confirmed by both our and their players. Our key player, Richard Mantell, (who later played regularly for England) summed up the match with unconscious irony. 'They were the best side we've thrashed all season.'

It has been a pleasure today to be able to appoint a part-time biology teacher called Joy Ride.

Amelia is, we think, at risk. She tells our counsellor Claire of a fight at home, which was stopped by police in the small hours. It also emerges that the family of eight lives in a two-bedroom house: Amelia and three sisters aged one to fourteen in one room, her older brother in the other, the parents downstairs, and a younger brother in a caravan. Food? Not last week, because father burnt the spaghetti. She says her siblings are frightened, although only the oldest boy has been hit so far. Tomorrow it's the Easter holiday. Many phone calls follow, mostly between Claire and the social services, to secure Amelia's safety for the next three weeks at least, after which we are going to have to find a boarding place for her somewhere.

James is being teased about being gay. To register his dismay, and presumably to force the issue into the open, the poor chap has stolen three wallets, which he laid out in a row, unopened in front of a security camera. Mother arrives to discuss the matter, but father does not join her. Indeed, it seems that he spends very little time with James.

'We all tease him about being gay at home. He's the odd one out,' she says, in front of her stricken son.

The last day of term. Four assemblies to celebrate all that has happened in the last few weeks, to award cups and prizes and generally to try to send everyone off feeling good about the many fine things they and others have achieved. Then Mrs K. comes from Moscow, tearfully pleading that I allow the dreaded Alexei back next term, though I have five quads this week alone demonstrating his refusal to attend classes and the extent of his malign influence on others. I have great sympathy for her for she is intensely vulnerable and I suspect even a little frightened of her son. His guardian assures me that his father will now assemble a posse of legal high-fliers to fight me over my decision to exclude the boy, but there is no alternative. The poor chap is spoilt beyond redemption here. I just hope for his mother's sake that he redeems himself elsewhere.

A colleague who has been interviewed for a job at Downside looks in to let me know how it went. When asked about his extra-curricular interests, he offered to take the shooting. The headmaster, Dom Antony Sutch, a good friend, had apparently replied with anticipatory glee, 'Oh good, I am sure we will be able to line up some Protestants for you to aim at.'

I have offered a bursary to Yoon-Mi from Korea, whose father faxes me, 'Dear C. S. Martin, How are you? I am happy that my lovely daughter can now stay at your esteemed school.' A large posse of her many friends come to see me before dispersing for the holiday to say how grateful they are that I have 'saved' her. At least I have done one thing right today, but what was it John Garnett used to say when he was Director of the Industrial Society? 'You cannot expect to earn a salary and get a round of applause.' I must not let their gratitude, gratifying though it is, go to my head.

That was on Friday. On the Sunday, we left at 5.50 a.m. on our last recruiting trip to Kuala Lumpur, Singapore, Jakarta, Brunei, Hong Kong, Macau and China, all in eleven days. I spoke at six receptions, met countless current and prospective parents and pupils, and generally waved the Millfield flag as hard as possible. The most touching moments were those involving saying goodbye to so many people whom we have got to know and like so much over the years—a foretaste of what is to come with retirement in the summer. In Jakarta, all the Indonesian parents gave us a splendid meal and then wheeled in a vast mahogany trunk, which they presented to us, before the youngsters kindly and most touchingly drove us to the airport to say their farewells. All this tended to give the lie to the picture of gloom painted by the FCO official information sheet on Indonesia: 'Current economic crisis...unrest...demonstrations...haze...respiratory problems... crime wave...swimming accidents...piracy...earthquakes...volcanic eruptions. Enjoy your holiday.'

In Hong Kong a Rolls Royce had been organized to meet us at Kai Tak by Paula and G. B. Ong, such a luxury even when you realize that there are more Rollers in Hong Kong per head than anywhere else in the world. They also gave us a sumptuous meal to say goodbye—the last sadness in the Far East before flying home to the UK, arriving at Heathrow to find our luggage was in Paris. Once back in Street, we could not get into the house because our keys were in Paris too! So we stood outside for half an hour in our thin tropical garb, in horizontal sleet, until help could be summoned, with the ambient temperature at just two degrees.

Chapter 9

A significant tree is planted

APRIL 1998. The first day of my last term. An excellent young teacher is first through the door with the news that he has accepted a post in Oxford. Our loss, their gain. He is one of some ten teachers here currently who, I'd wager, would become headteachers in due course if they wanted to go down that line. Then Tim Wilbur adds a splendid request for an early departure at half-term to play hockey for the GB Veterans side in the World Championships. The team apparently has to have eleven players whose combined ages total 440 years. The 1998 sculptor in residence, Chris Booth from New Zealand, is already hard at work on his eighteen tons of stone. The foundations for his piece will have to be massive and we have yet to decide where to erect it. It's going to be five meters high. But he has just secured the Greenham Common commission, so we know he is no slouch and clearly believes in impressively big projects.

The prefects are in good fettle, apart from Kohelika, who remains in Delhi with amoebic dysentery. They seem to enjoy my unguarded exhortation at the end of our meeting 'to go forth and multiply', before I hastily correct myself over the second injunction.

Every afternoon I see two or three prospective families together for half an hour after their tour to try to answer their queries about the school. I invariably enjoy these sessions, for our visitors are almost always inspired by what they have seen of us and have no difficulty in appreciating what we have to offer. Today, they wanted to talk about girls' dress, which I admitted was not my top priority, drug education, modular courses, racial mix, criteria for House placements, and the range of sixth-form courses available. All are entirely sensible and reveal well-briefed people who have followed developments in education for some time. And yet I sometimes long for the good old days when they used to ask whether I was in favour of capital punishment, ('No. We could not afford to lose the fees'), and league tables, though no one has mentioned these to me for a couple of years now.

Just two days into the new term and already we have a new variant on sexual obsession. The parents of a 14-year-old boy are concerned, with good reason, that the mother of one of his contemporaries has developed an unhealthy infatuation for him, writing to him often twice a day in the most inappropriate terms. I am shown some of her letters by way of illustration of what is going on. I assure them that we will try to protect their son, and indeed later talk on the phone to the mother concerned, but we cannot offer guarantees that the embarrassed boy will never again receive expressions of her devotion. Only a court injunction can achieve that.

Rob Wadsworth is to be seen practising football skills by himself on the Astro pitch for hours on end. He can bounce a ball on his feet, his head, his knee, his shoulders apparently endlessly. No wonder he has offers to compete for Southampton and Sampdoria. But it is his body swerve that is his secret weapon. He can convince his opponent, the spectators, the referee and even his own side that he's going one way, and then he goes the other.

It's the Upper Sixth photograph. There are 260 people in away-match dress and thirty tutors, all shepherded onto the stand in perfect height order. We are all adjusting our grins when the heavens open. It's a downpour and within seconds we are all soaked. We dash for cover to the swimming pool foyer, emerging five minutes later, when it has passed, to try again. Vicky 'the Voice' Turney suggests people will think we all smarm our hair down as some sort of institutional corporate fetish.

The first week ends with a day when there is no unscheduled time between 7.45 a.m. and 6.0 p.m. Thus it is not with unalloyed joy that I get home to find there is a mystery invitation that evening, of which it transpires Julia has known for some time. But on arrival at the Mullions it turns out to be the Senior Prefects who have organized a special dinner for us. Their welcome, their thoughtfulness and their exuberant company give more pleasure than they will probably ever know. It is an evening to treasure long into the depths of retirement.

Helen, in the Upper Sixth, and I find ourselves walking across the campus together, and I ask her how things are in her House. She is worried that, while she wants to help her juniors with their prep, she's not sure whether she should. And she has a further worry.

'I know what the real answers are in their history prep for instance, but I've forgotten what the fourth-year answers are supposed to be.'

This morning I enjoyed hearing the junior education minister say on the *Today* programme that she wanted 'all the bread and butter issues to be tackled on the ground.'

And this afternoon I enjoyed hearing our visiting speaker, a splendid Somerset farmer, talking on the future of agriculture, say, 'The only good sheep is a cooked sheep. All they do is die. And get out.' He held 350 fairly sophisticated young people in the palm of his hand for an hour because, as it seemed to me, he was such a complete person, without guile, and with a seductive sense of humour with which we could all readily identify.

Izam has hit his girl-friend and given her a black eye. He is suspended. Five minutes later, on his way out of school they pass me arm in arm, and greet me politely as if nothing had happened,

[159]

even though she is reduced to wearing dark glasses. We adults do have a tough time understanding teenage love.

The A-Level Theatre Studies group has produced twelve 'A's and two 'B's, but the examiner, an experienced woman, declares their group project the best she has ever seen. She also awards Vicky the Voice full marks, the first time this has been heard of. Surely we will see her name in lights one day, if this is what she wants—and if her splendid, deep voice holds out.

There is also news that we have two physicists in the top sixteen in the country in the British Physics Olympiad; Feng Gao and Yueyang Zhao. Two other Beijing pupils collect a Silver (top 100) and a Bronze (top 250) award.

It is the BMC Open Athletics meeting, with a galaxy of international runners on our track all evening. Carl Myerscough competes with the shot. He throws 30 centimetres further than the previous British record, but the shot hits the board and cannot be counted. I commiserate with him afterwards.

'You must be disappointed?'

'Oh no Sir, I only came down this evening for a training session. I'm really quite pleased.'

Kernick House—our weekly house visit. Two fifth-form girls who have been extremely tiresome for two years, but who seem now to have grown up quite a bit, impress me that they could yet become successful sixth-formers. Optimism surges within my ageing breast and I tell them so.

They beam and chat about their selection for the first girls' cricket fixture at the weekend at Blundell's. 'Our first off-lessons chit ever, Sir.'

Sadly, the very next day, with my endorsement of their new maturity possibly still lurking somewhere in their subconscious, they are seen in a pub in Street. Suspension is inevitable. Goodbye sixth-form hopes and goodbye cricket selection. I am really sorry for them and learn belatedly to moderate my faith in human nature.

Walking round the campus on a glorious Sunday afternoon, I bump into Tatiphon Teparagul from Thailand who has been here since the third-form. She has a place to read Maths at Cambridge and a black belt in Karate. I am not surprised by the first achievement but, given her diminutive size—I could probably pick her up with one hand—I am most impressed by the second. I ask her what quality you need to be really good at Karate. Without hesitation, she replies, 'Spirit, Sir'.

A note from a houseparent. 'During Sunday playtime, David thought it a good idea to cover his dorm-mate's face with chocolate and to try to wash it off with a fire extinguisher. Shades of David Mellor, but unlike the politician, this David is to be gated for a week.'

I have just appointed to the PE department David Hacker, the current Welsh hockey captain, who must miss the first weeks in September to compete in the Commonwealth Games. With Alan Lerwill, former England jumper, sprinter and record holder, Richard Ellison, former England cricketer, Adrian Simcox, former Scottish tennis coach and Doug Campbell, who is a GB swimming coach, we do seem to have a strong coaching team.

A roller-coaster day today, which happily starts with the arrival of Mike Absalom, a wonderfully good-natured prefect, who delivers a petition with 500 signatures of boys of all ages, urging me not to make ties compulsory with shirt sleeve order. Of such stuff are the barricades made upon which the young will hurl themselves today! His approach was so civilized that I had not the heart to disappoint him, so ties will remain optional after all. Is this weakness or good sense? I convince myself it is a question of *reculer pour mieux sauter*.

A hurried visit to Sherborne for my last HMC meeting after nineteen years with the South West division; sadly an unusually dull affair with everyone clearly pretty jaded as the year struggles to an end. All this was transformed, however, on my return for the House Athletics finals—my favourite event of the year. The sun shone, the whole school was out in force around the track, and the support was loud and generous as Carl Myerscough threw a new Junior British shot record, beating 21 metres for the first time; Ed Willers cleared 2.15 metres in the high jump, and Hilary Vince bravely completed the 1500 metres to earn points for her House, even though suffering from asthma. Eight records were beaten in half an hour. And at the end all the litter was cleared up. Finally, a relaxed hour with Peter Johnson who was down to appoint his Head of PE for next year, and the evening spent touring Joan's Kitchen in a thunderstorm. The day rounded off at 1.30 a.m. by the news of the birth of our grandson in London, also in a thunderstorm. Heady stuff!

Many parents have as much to learn as their children, and sometimes more. Two letters today illustrate this. The first is from an educated couple whose son is in constant minor trouble. Last term we sat down together and worked out agreed targets for him in what we all saw as a probationary term. These were all spelled out carefully on paper and the boy's parents and I went through them carefully with him. Now the boy is suspended for drinking, and the parents, neatly forgetting all that has gone before, resort to personal abuse of me. The second is from the mother of a girl who is reprimanded and gated for swearing and throwing her racket in a tennis match. Instead of apologizing for her errant daughter, she tries to blame games staff for punishing her. I have always tried to be temperate in my replies to aggrieved parents, and generally, when this proves difficult, I have asked them to come in and discuss their grievances with me. In both these cases, however, I let fly. Perhaps I am becoming demob happy.

A girl is defaulted for being improperly dressed. She's very pretty, knows it and, as a fully signed up 15-year-old, is not above trying to exploit her looks with anyone who might prove susceptible. This time however she resorts to a letter to her housemaster which he finds on his desk at the end of break.

Dear Mr Warne,

I went to the staff room and waited for ages but sadly—obviously—our paths did not cross. Anyway, I have to go to my lesson now. What I wanted to tell you was that my shirt was in my bag. It was there because a fourth-year flicked poster paint at me in first period. As it is Janice's shirt, I had to try to wash it out immediately. I've even left the shirt for you here to see it's the truth, risking being defaulted by all the other teachers for being late, but I suppose I have no choice otherwise you may not believe me.

     Juliet

P.S. Mr Harper was there too so you could ask him.

P.P.S. As you can see it's unwearable.

In the category of excuse concoction, this is clearly worth a Nobel Prize. It is so good that we have no difficulty in agreeing not to default her at all.

Just before a cycling expedition for the third form, a note is found and handed in by a sympathetic tutor. 'Dear God, please let my cycling trip be brilliant. Lots of love from Will.'

I am concerned for the families of our seven Indonesian Chinese pupils as news comes through that parts of Jakarta are being torched by a mob and that they are specifically targeting Chinese concerns. Fiona Haribowo comes to reassure me. Her brother has spoken to their father who says that none of his friends is hurt, although some of their property has been pillaged. She feels things are easing now, but I find it hard to share her optimism.

The third-year assembly this morning featured an excellent presentation by about twenty of them, highlighting in a number of imaginative scenes the need to start to plan a strategy towards a choice of career now, and introducing next year's structured careers programme. In view of my forthcoming job interviews, my ears prick up and I'm sure I listen as attentively as anyone.

The security guard told me this morning how last night he had watched as a vixen led four fox cubs out from under the Bolts and let them play in the moonlight on the headmaster's lawn, right in the middle of the campus.

Claire, our counsellor, has had a major operation and we are all hugely relieved to know that it has gone well. After a week on a drip, she is now eating again. Apparently her granddaughter Sophie, aged four, tried to call her at the hospital. She got through to the front desk and said, 'May I speak to my granny please?'

The receptionist naturally needed a little more to work on and asked, 'Which granny is that?' To which Sophie apparently replied with asperity, 'I've only got one granny.'

The golfers are in ecstasy today as Ernie Els flies in for the day in his helicopter, accompanied by a posse of Sky TV people and other journalists. He turns out to be a delightful young chap, huge, and with a natural touch with our youngsters. He wanted to see everything from the pool to the library, so Camilla and Kim took him round and charmed him to bits. He had a game of tennis and got twenty of our golfers to drive off from the range under his eagle eye. He thought they stood up to the pressure of doing this on TV remarkably well.

An epic game of cricket between the newly formed Senior girls' team and the Foals C team, some of which I was lucky enough to see. The boys posted their highest score of the season—80 all out on the last ball of their allotted overs. The girls clearly scented victory but in the event their game plan foundered on dodgy preparation. They admitted that they had 'done' bowling and fielding but had unfortunately omitted to 'do' batting. Thus they were all out for 30, despite some impressive chivalry from the little boys, who offered tactful advice on how to avoid being lbw and judiciously dropped a number of gifted catches in the slips. Perhaps they feared that the senior girls might issue detentions for over zealous fielding. It was touching to see these mature young women bending down to shake hands with their opponents at the end of the game.

Peter Mills, a senior houseparent, is whisked into hospital with a heart episode, his pulse leaping wildly from 60 to 180. Vicky, his wife, calls when we get back from the Summer Ball, having stopped off to watch the fox cubs playing on the lawn. He is quite seriously ill and there is cause for real alarm, mitigated slightly by Peter's characteristically laconic appreciation of the ministrations of his nurse, who rejoices in the name of Nigel.

The next morning, with half-term starting after lunch, I have to send a girl away for smoking cannabis. Her parent was belligerent and searched wildly around for people to blame, attributing no responsibility to his daughter, who has certainly had her chances with us already. When parents ask about the level of drug involvement here, I try to convey to them not only the inevitable attraction to the young of forbidden fruit, but also the fact that the hit rate of discovery in any school is dependent as much on the vigilance of the staff and their determination not to turn a blind eye, as it is on the proclivities of the youngsters themselves. I know only one Head who was foolish enough to state publicly that there were no drugs in her school. I also know of several where the Head would admit privately that the school would empty if random drug testing were introduced. Prefects assure me that pupils at least know where they stand in this regard here, and I believe them.

At lunchtime, as if to cheer us all up, four rock bands play in the quad in the sunshine. These include the incomparable Becky Hanson, a fourth-form girl with a very striking voice and totally convincing presentation who surely has a really good chance of making it big time in the music world. It occurs to me that if I play my cards right, I might be able to persuade her to engage me as her agent after the summer. She certainly has a future, and I understand that recording companies are already beginning to hover.

Half-term, and it is time for me to do a final trip overseas to represent Millfield abroad. This time it's to the USA where I am to visit our Millfield Fellow coordinator at the University of Virginia, and attend a reunion for Old Millfieldians in New York. First however, I'm due to spend a day in the University of North Carolina with the staff of the Morehead Foundation, for whom I interview scholarship candidates in London from time to time. I leave Street for Heathrow in a taxi with Nadia, who is returning to Kiev for the week. Our driver is Paul, who tells us with alarming equanimity how he was invalided out of the police having been run over by a truck while grappling with an armed robber. The transatlantic flight is uneventful as always, though I am left wondering why American Airlines cabin staff have been instructed, as they plainly have been, to avoid all eye contact with their passengers. During the flight, I also come to terms with the fact that over there, a bar of soap is known as a clarifying bar.

This information does not really prepare me, however, for the taxi driver who takes me from Raleigh to Chapel Hill. He seems pretty low, so I ask him how he is. To my horror, he bursts into floods of tears and explains, sobbing, that his wife has thrown him out and that none of his beloved daughters will talk to him, and would I please talk to his oldest daughter on his mobile to try to woo her round to allow him to visit her. With that, he dials the number and passes me the phone, and a surreal conversation takes place.

'Hello, you don't know me but I'm sitting in your father's cab and you need to know how very fond he is of you...'

She mellows after a while and I pass the phone back to her father. The cab stops on the hard shoulder—the clock is still ticking, I notice—and a lengthy, moving reconciliation takes place between them. Such is the effect of this on my driver, that eventually he delivers me free of charge to my hotel, overwhelmed by what he takes to be my counselling skills. It seems like a propitious start to my trip.

While digesting the low-down on the Morehead empire with Megan Mazzochi, the ebullient key to the success of the scholarship scheme, it is entertaining to learn that the first woman President of UNC is called Molly Broad, and that her Vice President is a Mr Hooker.

Another taxi back to the airport, this time in the hands of a basketball fanatic. He found it necessary to change lanes repeatedly in order to demonstrate to me, as graphically as the confined space of his taxi would allow, the moves made by Michael Jordan which enabled him to change hands in mid-air while heading for the basket. It was only at the airport, when I found it hard to unclench my colourless knuckles, that I realized how exciting the demonstration had been. Thence to Washington, where I changed into a sort of flying minibus. As the small group of passengers clambered into the plane, the pilot, who had his feet up in the cockpit reading the paper, asked with genuine curiosity where we wanted to go.

'Charlottesville? Sure, that's cool. I guess I can find Charlottesville. But you know it's windy up there today, so we'll stick low in the white water.' With that, he unfolded a road map of the way to Charlottesville, spread it out on his knees and we took off. A piece of cake.

Discussions on the future of the Virginia Fellowship scheme went well, and both sides recognize the success of the four graduates who have already done their year with us at Millfield, contributing so much to the international flavour of the school. Rachel, next year's Fellow, took me out to Monticello putting me in touch again with Jefferson, one of my life-long heroes. Every detail of the house and its gardens seems to point up the unique innovative genius of the man. Not many of us could declare with such confidence that 'A gentleman should be able to tie an artery, dance a minuet and play the violin.'

My next taxi to Charlottesville airport is driven by Dot Ebbins. She is so large that she takes up one and a half of the front two seats and I have no option but to sit behind, from where there is only a very restricted view of the road ahead. She turns out to be 76 years old, and she smokes 50 cigarettes a day. Looking at the floor of her cab, this does not surprise me. She admits that she and her doctor do not get on. 'Ma doctor don like me comin' through his door, so I don go no mo.'

A vulture, poised on a post at the end of the runway, sees us off on our return to Washington in another diminutive plane. Does it know more about these trips than we do? In New York, Behdad Alizadeh had made all the arrangements for the annual reunion of the NY branch of the Old Millfieldians and some twenty people showed up. They were most welcoming and I enjoyed their company, but with only a couple of months still in post, I am seen as history, I suspect, and their interest in recent developments at Millfield is consequently somewhat limited.

The second half of the term starts with the emotional temperature immediately turned right up. Anna is in dire straights. There has been self-harm, a threat of suicide, a string of dress and games defaulters and two smoking offences in the week back from suspension. She tells us repeatedly that she hates her mother and that her father never speaks to her. She insists that she wants nothing more than to be with her friends at school and yet she pushes the self-destruct button as soon as she is back from the mid-term holiday. I call her mother to let her know why we can no longer be responsible for her while fulfilling our obligations to others in her House and in her classes. Mother has no difficulty in blaming us for everything, and yet describes her daughter as being schizophrenic. She insists that relations within the family are harmonious, and it is tempting to tell her what her daughter has told us of them, but it would do no good for poor Anna. It reminds me of John Rae's exhortation to parents at Westminster when he was headmaster there: 'If you promise not to believe everything your children tell you about us, I promise not to believe everything they tell us about you.'

But this highlights the most pernicious difficulty with which we are so often faced when dealing with confidences. Pupils say things of importance which we are not allowed to mention to parents. Parents say things which they want kept secret from their children. Colleagues overhear conversations between pupils in classrooms which may or may not have been intentionally held within earshot and yet cannot divulge names, and so on. And as often as not I find myself pig in the middle, burdened with confidences on all sides and sometimes liable to confuse which bits of whose meetings I'm supposed to know about and which I'm not. It's all part of the job, of course, but such constraints do act as a powerful brake on the construction of solutions. When he was in charge of the Inner London Education Authority, Peter Newsome once said that ILEA had 'the engine of a lawn-mower and the brakes of a juggernaut truck.' Trying to negotiate the minefield of confidences which characterizes so many teenage issues often reminds me of how he felt.

Connor is gated for a minor drinking offence. He is a pleasant Irish lad in the Lower Sixth. His mother returns my call and is furious with him. She believes no one should have any access to alcohol at all, even in controlled circumstances at home, until they are 18 years old. She roundly condemns me for allowing sixth-formers into a supervised school bar on a handful of Saturday evenings each term. There are two different cultures at work here which it is impossible to bridge. Connor, poor chap, was too frightened to tell his parents of his peccadillo over half-term, leaving it to me to tell them now. They are threatening to remove him from the school. This would not serve him at all well and would surely be a gross over-reaction in these circumstances.

Dinos, who left a couple of years ago, came back to visit us today. He is now playing hooker for Wasps, having lost two stone. Which means he has come right down to 16 stone—a formidable spectacle for the opposition front row in the scrum. In his delightfully diffident way, he describes how, having played now in most of the major stadiums in England, he gets more of a *frisson* of excitement stepping onto our Jubilee pitch than anywhere else, even in summer when the posts are missing.

Last week the 1st XI scored 175 for 5 and declared a bit late against Eton, who were 126 for 8 at the close. This week, the Free Foresters did the same thing to us, but happily we went for the runs nevertheless. We eventually needed four off the last ball with our last batsmen at the crease. We were all out and lost the match, but what a relief that we were not guilty of battening down the hatches and grinding out a dreary draw. I am much prouder of our people for their loss, earned in such dynamic fashion.

Earlier, we had beaten Harrow in a round of the Lord's Taverners Trophy.

I happened to be around as they were heading for their coach and was surprised to be asked by their pleasant master in charge, 'Headmaster, do any of your boys go on to University?'

I didn't like to ask him if Harrow had sent twenty-eight pupils to Oxbridge last year as we had, for I'm pretty sure it would have proved embarrassing for him. However, his question did underline the fact that we are still not seen as a serious academic institution, even by those swimming in the same pool, and I must take a good deal of the responsibility for this failure.

Max in the fourth-year comes up to me on the athletics track and tells me he likes my portrait, which hangs in the current summer exhibition. 'A really good composition,' he says with feeling.

'Oh good,' say I, 'Have you seen the other picture there by the same artist?'

Max looks blank.

'You know,' I prod his memory, 'the one of the girl in her bra with a bloke standing close behind her?'

For a moment then, I realize I have his complete, unadulterated attention, and even I suspect, his respect. His mouth opens. Breath comes out, and then, 'Was that you as well, Sir?'

In an idle moment, I run through the names of all the Heads of School I've appointed in the last eight years. There are forty-eight of them, a boy and a girl each term. To my surprise, when I start to think about them all as a group, I realize that a quite disproportionate number are dyslexic. What can account for this? I recall the classes I have taught in which dyslexic pupils predominate and am again aware of the extent to which they thrive on group activities, reaching out to others for all the help they can get, rather than struggling away by themselves. They are among the best communicators, therefore, and are often born team players—qualities which have obviously given them the edge when we are looking for people who will win respect on the strength of their personalities, rather than merely on account of their promotion. I wonder how I can convey this generally *pour encourager les autres*?

I bump into Ben, who is in the fifth-form, and who decides to get something off his chest.

'I really want to succeed here, Sir. I've tried hard in classes. My games are going well. I think I might even make the 1st XV next term, and in the House I volunteer all the time, and I've taken Mr and Mrs Gabb's children to the shops and everything. And now they are moving to your new House, Sir, and I've got new houseparents. It's not fair. Three years of creeping wasted!'

This is followed by a two hour Executive group meeting to determine the minor capital bids for next year. As usual, Paul has prepared it all meticulously. We consider over fifty suggestions, both our own and those submitted by staff. They range from a new digital phone system for the whole school, to a school yacht. We have £1.1 million to spend, but some individual projects costing twice as much have been put forward. There is certainly no lack of imagination or ambition among colleagues.

This afternoon, I saw three very different sets of parents all together. They were an Indonesian couple, three generations of Russian women supporting a little girl so small that I felt I could pick her up with one finger, and the Kuwaiti Ambassador to London. They all got on tremendously well, having done the tour of the school together with two pupils. I hardly needed to say anything at all, for they were too busy telling each other how much they had enjoyed everything they had seen and heard. When prospective parents sell the school to each other like this, the headmaster rapidly becomes entirely redundant.

The next morning was not a good one. By the time the mid-morning break arrived to put me out of my misery, four pupils had been presented to me in one way or another, none of whom merited congratulation. First there was Jihad who lost his temper last night in his boarding house and started smashing furniture with a hockey stick. The story goes that back home he had broken the arm of someone who had tried to pacify him when he was in comparable mode, so his housemaster and senior boys had had to employ endless patience and diplomacy to talk him down this time round. Clearly he can only be allowed to stay on if room can be found for him in a billet. There will be no more boarding house life for him here in future.

Then came Jane, who had been found stealing in the Girls' Cottage where they all leave their school clothes when doing games. This is serious, for nothing makes people feel more vulnerable in a close community than theft, with the attendant sense that they are being watched and preyed upon for any oversight in their care of their possessions. Eventually we called the police, though even then she only admitted her offences after twenty minutes of lies and evasion. She will now have a long suspension and will be readmitted only on very strict conditions.

Next came Julia, who flouts our dress code persistently and has started to remonstrate with tutors who patiently, or nowadays not so patiently, try to correct her. Her defiance means that she really cannot now return to the sixth-form next year. When I put this to her, reminding her of the long string of examples of tiresome and uncooperative behaviour which have brought us to this point, she is outraged and accuses me bitterly of being petty minded. Perhaps she is right, but her refusal to meet us even half way, and her current defiance of colleagues leave me no alternative. But I am sorry she will be going, all the same.

And finally the depressing news that Helen, suspended in March for bulimia, with its devastating effect on those around her, is vomiting while at home up to seven times a day. She tells us her mother has no idea of this at all. Her illness is profound and requires intensive medical attention. It is mortifying that such a very gifted and delightful person should still be a prey to such a very debilitating condition.

The day is retrieved in the afternoon by Mark Cook's stirring presentation on Hope and Homes for Children, and the pupils' heartfelt response to him. He is a fellow former Gurkha officer, who was so moved by the plight of orphans he encountered in Bosnia that he has spent his life since in developing a charity to support them, both there and elsewhere. Jo Edwards then invited me to attend her after-school activity as a client. It was Stretching and Relaxation. I found myself one of a class of twenty pupils, all of whom were bending themselves into all sorts of amazing contortions, while I remained as stiff as a board. But it was good to have been asked, and I did rediscover bits of my anatomy that I had forgotten about for years.

And then today, the ultimate nightmare. Jen, celebrating her fourteenth birthday with some illicit vodka, fell off the flat roof of her boarding house and was killed. Nothing, of course, prepares you for such a thing. My memories of that terrible afternoon seem like a silent film. I can see it all vividly in my mind's eye but there seems to be no sound. Everything appears strangely disembodied. And yet I talked with Jen's marvellous houseparents, Doc and Jo, so shocked and yet so aware of their duty to others. I talked with the police, with the other girls in Johnson's, with Hugh, our doctor, and the staff in the medical centre, with the girl who shared Jen's room and with her parents, with Jen's brother Tim in Joan's Kitchen, and with Jen's parents in Singapore who were making plans to fly over that night. I talked with senior colleagues about arranging additional cover for the girls in the House that night to enable Doc and Jo to come and stay with us to recover a little. They had spent time that morning with Jen, wishing her a happy birthday and so on, and were distraught. I talked with others about the best time to present the news to colleagues and to the pupils and about preparing a statement for the press. And I talked with Simon, our chaplain, and Mr Gelardi, Jen's grandfather, and with Tim again when they both came that night to our house for supper. Finally I talked with Richard Voisey, our incomparable local taxi driver, who readily agreed at no notice to drive Simon and Mr Gelardi to Heathrow to meet Jen's parents off their flight early the next morning.

And all the time, through to midnight and beyond, all the talking and the making of arrangements, and the attempted comforting of others seemed to be coming from someone else. I did not quite recognize myself. I knew of course that things would never be the same again, but I could not figure out how, or even for whom. Except of course in respect to her family.

That night, when the talking stopped temporarily, I confronted for the first time the horror of what had happened. I knew her parents quite well and liked them a lot. I had met her father first in Jakarta and remembered exactly where we sat at that meeting and even pretty much what we said. We had got on well from the outset, with the result that Tim was entered for Millfield and Jen followed him a couple of years later. Julia and I had met Anne, Jen's mother, at the reunion in Singapore just three months ago. And now they were on a ten-hour flight, not even knowing whether Jen was indeed dead or not, though the doctor at the hospital who had spoken to them before they left had, I think, held out little hope at that stage. And I was responsible. Not directly perhaps, but ultimately. What was I to say to them in the morning? What on earth could I say to them?

Sunday became Monday. The hospital, senior staff at 8, letters to governors, others to parents of the girls in Johnson's, then over to the medical centre to see Pippa, who had been with Jen shortly before she fell. She was still too traumatised to talk, but her parents had come down from the north and they were angry. A terrible conversation, but during the course of the day they began to realize the level of support that was being offered to Pippa and were big enough to express appreciation. Crossing the road back onto the campus the first TV cameras zoomed in and the battle with the media began. I talked to the staff at break, to the third-year group tutors separately and to the whole of Jen's year immediately afterwards. Such desperate distress. We arranged for candles to be available in the chapel for those who wanted to light them, and we opened a book of condolence, which started to fill up very fast

And then the moment I knew I had been dreading most of all, when Paul and Anne arrived in the taxi from the airport. Simon had met them and broken the confirmation of Jen's death to them. They were amazing. The first thing they wanted to know was how the other girls were, and whether they were very upset. And then Paul lifted a colossal part of the burden from my shoulders when he said, 'Jen always regarded rules as being merely advisory.'

I could not have been more grateful to him. They came home for lunch with Julia and me. We talked of Jen and Tim, but of other things too, and then went round to the chapel. There were probably a dozen people there from Jen's year. Alli, who is in Johnson's and knew Jen well, recognized her mother and presented her with some flowers that she was about to place on the altar. It was a most graceful gesture, a poignant moment even, given the emotional turmoil of the whole context.

Minutes later there were eight TV, press and live radio interviews on the trot, before a return to Pippa and her stricken parents in the medical centre. I had to cut this short to welcome 150 new parents who had come for a reception, prior to their children's arrival in September. Just as I was bracing myself to launch myself on an occasion which seemed infinitely removed from the reality of the last two days, two tear-stained girls came rushing up.

'Sir, we've lit so many votive candles that we've set the chapel on fire.'

And they had. When I arrived, the fire engine was already there. Typical Millfield. Do nothing by halves. If you're going to light a candle, do it in style. Set fire to the chapel. I went back to the parents in a more positive mood than had seemed possible just ten minutes earlier and started my spiel to them by saying what had just happened. They were already aware of yesterday's tragedy. I told them how proud I was to be part of a school whose staff and senior pupils had demonstrated such sky-high levels of concern and support for the bereft juniors all day. Millfield at her best. We will be vilified by the press in the days ahead, no doubt, but we have seen on the campus today all the hallmarks of a really vibrant community, one which few of us have the privilege of sharing. True institutional and personal strength have been revealed, of which we might not have become aware, but for the trigger of calamity in the shape of Jen's loss. These have been the most emotionally extenuating days of my life. And the trauma is still in its infancy.

Over 200 of Jen's contemporaries came to her Requiem Mass in Glastonbury. Her father and grandfather attended. The sun shone, Simon gave a wonderful homily and people then came home for coffee. The book in the chapel has attracted many entries, some short, most long, and all extremely personal. The proportion of girls to boys who have written in it must be about ten to one. Support levels are still high, staff and pupils drawing on each other's strength. The only relieving feature of the whole day, which

I am rather ashamed to have spotted, was during the reading in the church. We had just got to the clarion call, 'And I heard a voice from Heaven saying...', when a telephone rang loudly in the vestry. It was just like a hot-line. Rather reassuring really.

Life seems to go on. There are after all still three weeks to go and there are still 1,250 children to care for. Two quads bring relief. This one was from Giles Neeve, who turns the average routine report into a minor work of art: 'Robert has been smoking and lying abed in the mornings, though not simultaneously, I hasten to add. He is driving his housemaster to drink. I may soon follow. I shall write to his poor long-suffering mum. Action: one week school detention. I shall enjoy his company.'

And by the same post another from the same source.

'I was sitting down to eat last night—chicken casserole as it happens—when I was called to the phone and was ambushed by Mrs N. in her most truculent, no-surrender mode. All had been arranged for her son in the unusual clash between physics and tennis—uneasy bedfellows at the best of times—to his complete satisfaction. He said he understood the solution to the problem. Not so mater. I vented some subdued spleen. The conversation ended.'

Two girls have just come to see me. They have been on the rack for three days, poor people, for it was they who had used false ID to obtain the vodka for Jen. The burden they feel now is clearly almost intolerable. But what on earth could have possessed them? They did not know Jen, so there was no misplaced bond of friendship which could have prompted them to act so irresponsibly. They are respectively the most reliable and the quietest person you could ever encounter. I have been teaching one of them this term, and eliciting any verbal response from her was harder than getting funds out of Fort Knox. I tried to encourage them, but we all agreed that I had no option but to inform the police, who will need to take statements from them both. This is a most unwelcome development, highlighting the ease with which ID can be forged even by the least criminal youngsters.

The press has been fairly subdued on the issue. Twelve nationals have carried the news of Jen's death with *The Sun*, the *Daily Star* and the *Mail* at the bottom end of the scale but with sensitive reporting from the broadsheets and even from the *Express*. But the underlying hypocrisy is heavy in the nostrils and the inaccuracies too many to enumerate. Have they really no idea that young people today, as always, seek to experiment, to take risks, to break rules both at home and at school, and indeed everywhere in between? Were the editors and reporters themselves never young? Is it supposed to indicate something significant that, as one paper reports, I expelled four pupils for drugs in 1996? And if so, what? That we are more alert than many schools to the danger of drugs and more rigorous than many in our treatment of those who become involved? I doubt that that is the point they are trying to underscore somehow. And what is this reference to LSD? There has been no such reported case in the eight years I have been here. Perhaps they have dredged it up from the '60s? The pupils are outraged by such gratuitous inaccuracy.

Cuong Do Lenh comes to say goodbye. He's just finished his last A Level and returns home to Hanoi tonight, for the first time since he arrived two years ago. Next stop Balliol to read maths. I remember the first time I met him in a bleak classroom in Hanoi–Amsterdam school, one of the most selective schools in the country. Sixty to a class with precious few resources, but clearly the standard of instruction was quite exceptional. He has certainly justified his full-fees scholarship!

It is Friday in the week of Jen's death. Five of the longest days any of us has known. It's the fourth-form assembly, when, from out of the blue, I am presented with a huge card signed by all 240 of them and a picture of Millfield House drawn by Stuart Lynch. As if that was not enough, Rebecca Hanson, whose name will be up in lights in due course, sang me a song in front of them all, accompanied by her band, and they all clapped. It was very stirring stuff, but my emotions this week are all over the place and I doubt that I was able sufficiently to show my real appreciation of their thoughtfulness. Fortunately I did not embarrass them or myself by shedding the tears that come easily just now.

Later in the day the normal routine was interrupted by the scheduled arrival of King Hussein's only sister, HRH Princess Basma Bint Talal, her husband His Excellency Walid Al-Kurdi, their children Saad and Zein, and two aides. A perceptive and charming woman, brilliant at putting people at their ease while clearly making a very thorough appreciation of what was going on around her. Saad appeared sublimely unspoilt, which in King Hussein's family, is not unexpected.

Saturday, the day of Jen's funeral in Weybridge where the bulk of her extended family live. Julia and I left at 7.30 with Daisy Lilley who was to play her recorder, and Alli Oyston, who would play her violin, both from Jen's House. Others from the House went up with various members of staff. Paul, her father, introduced the service with such consummate grace and dignity that for a fleeting moment I was tempted to think that all was all right with the world, that things were as they should be. But not for long. Bev Hatwell and I read and Simon again did the homily. We must all be asking ourselves over and over again, 'What if...?' 'If only...'. Then the burial, and the reception in the garden of Jen's uncle's house. Paul and Anne really are the most exceptional people. They are concerned for the rest of us, when the pain inflicted on them is so disproportionately greater.

Coming back in the car, first Simon and then the youngsters fall fast asleep. They have been the most draining six days imaginable. Dear God, six days! It feels like six weeks. And all the time I am trying to brace myself to leave this place in just a fortnight.

Things cannot get worse but they do. The police suddenly materialize in my room. The Health and Safety Executive have, they say, rethought their position. Whereas before they had declared themselves happy that all reasonable precautions, consistent with the requirements of the Fire Officer, had been taken to prevent girls climbing out onto the roof from which Jen fell, now they suggest that we may be guilty of 'recklessness'. They think we should have placed bars on the window, even though the Fire Officer had designated it officially as the second essential exit from the room, and had thus forbidden the addition of bars. Another investigation is to be launched, led by a CID inspector, with possible criminal charges at the end of it all. If found guilty of charges of corporate manslaughter, the police explained that the governors and I might find ourselves facing lengthy prison sentences. Fortunately Sir Robin, the Chairman of Governors happens to be in the room with me when they arrive and is immensely reassuring. I would not have wanted to receive such a visit alone at that point in this most emotionally charged week.

There is no time to brood on this turn of events, however, for a string of scheduled meetings still occur, the usual flurry of telephone calls still come in, and I try to compile a detailed letter to 2,000 parents in the middle of all this to explain to them exactly what has happened and what we are doing about it. Happily, the other members of the Gang of Four turn up for lunch, the Heads of Marlborough, Bryanston and Clifton, three pals on whom I can rely to understand exactly what all this feels like from my point of view. They don't let me down, and indeed the first of over fifty letters from other headmasters and headmistresses are arriving now, expressing heartfelt sympathy and often saying 'There but for the grace of God...'. They all know that any school, but particularly any boarding school, lives from day to day with the knowledge that teenage experimentation can go wrong at any time.

And then in the middle of everything it's time for today's group of prospective parents to grill me. It is a surreal combination—the sort of coalescence of cultures which could perhaps only happen at Millfield. They turn out to be a business man from the Central African Republic with a Pakistani aide, the Kazakhstani Ambassador to

Switzerland with an Indian aide and, in the midst of them, a pleasant but bemused English family who, it transpires, has only infrequently left Somerset, and who clearly think they have mistakenly arrived at the United Nations HQ. Happily, they all find lots to talk about following their tour and all leave in high spirits, chatting away as if they had known each other all their lives. I love that sort of thing. Having said goodbye to them outside, I was relieved to see that there were fewer young girls hanging about outside Reception than there had been yesterday, when Pierce Brosnan, complete with two long pigtails, had pitched up with his son.

In the last week of term we plant a tree on the campus near Jen's House, with a small plaque giving her name and dates. It's a low key affair but thirty or forty pupils attend all the same. I say something about the fact that the dates themselves are enough to demonstrate to pupils in the future that something shocking happened and that perhaps we should take away with us the thought that life is to be lived to the full. And then we just stand around in silence for some time until people start to drift away to other pressing things that claim them in the last week of a busy term.

There is little time for reflection as my career in teaching moves into its final weeks. For eight years I have given everything I have to Millfield, in terms of time of course—I was paid for that—but particularly in terms of emotional commitment. It would only be later that I would begin to realize the extent to which my almost single-minded involvement had jeopardized my relationship with my own children, grown up though they were by then. Throughout this time I've been conscious of my good fortune in being involved at the very heart of such a vibrant, innovative community. I've often literally pinched myself to make sure I really value my luck in having what I have always seen as the best job in education. So I have not been looking forward to saying goodbye to the school, and already envy my successor. I feel—perhaps self-indulgently—that I have many good friends on the staff and there have been remarkably few of the

4,000 pupils whom I've seen here whose company I do not welcome. I have enjoyed almost all my time here, but sense that I am now getting tired, and that the school will flourish in new hands. Thus it was not really a hard decision, last year, to turn down Sir Robin's generous offer that I might stay on for a couple of years longer.

But the nightmare of Jen's death hangs like a black cloud over these last two weeks and transforms what I had assumed would be a series of goodbyes, with all the pain and pleasure such things involve, into a functional business of trying to keep on top of what must be done on a daily basis while trying to ease the school's hurt at her loss. I receive plenty of support myself in this, mostly from other Heads, and open just one articulate, impassioned letter from a current parent, accusing me among other things of behaving more like a public relations man than like a headmaster. This hurts of course, but I feel almost numb by now and just hope that colleagues and pupils would disagree with him.

The end of term comes. The marquee goes up. Three thousand chairs are laid out in it. Exhibitions are prepared for Parents' Day, the last day of term. The grounds staff are busy putting the finishing touches to the campus. The athletes and cricketers are preparing for major events. The kitchens are full of activity as lunch is prepared for around 3,000 people, the pupils rush around being young, with the smell of the summer holidays in their nostrils, and teachers finish writing reports and seeing their tutees individually about them. The senior year, all 240 of them, are drifting back from post-exam leave and packing up their things ready for their ultimate departure.

I feel redundant and drift around like a ghost at someone else's feast. On the penultimate day I have three important speeches to make. There are goodbyes to be said in the Staff Common Room to the dozen or so teachers who are leaving with me. I work hard on these for it's so easy to be too dry, or too hearty, or to forget to mention that contribution to which a particular teacher has committed him or herself most enthusiastically. The Common Room, through their chairman, who like the rest of us is uninspired at this end of the term, give me a present. The chairman, to my mystification, then mentions that I have been good at curricular reform, something I have always left to the real professionals. Do they really know me so little? Have I really made no bigger impact than this on my colleagues? I'll probably never know.

Then there's the prize-giving in the marquee for the whole school. This goes well and is never a hard task, for everyone is in a good mood and ready to laugh at any half decent joke. And anyway, congratulating the young on their prodigious achievements is a genuine privilege and cannot in any case be done too passionately or too often. Rather to my dismay, my Deputy Head fails to say anything about my leaving, but he has other things on his mind no doubt. Schools are just not very good about saying goodbye to their Heads. Perhaps because after a while Heads are taken pretty much for granted by their schools. I think of the old saying: 'In your first year you can do no wrong. In your second you can do no good. And from then on no one cares very much what you do.' One or two colleagues do take the trouble to say goodbye personally, and I value their thoughtfulness greatly, even when they make the mistake of suggesting that my successor will not be as good as I have been. This is kind, but rubbish, for a number of obvious reasons. The story springs to mind of the elderly parishioner saying the same thing to her retiring priest, 'Your successor won't be as good as you, Father.'

'Oh yes, I'm sure he will,' replies the priest, though quietly gratified by the sentiment.

'No, he won't. I've seen five priests through this parish and each one has been worse than the last.'

After lunch, it's time to give the prep school prizes away, also for the last time. The sun shines brightly, everyone is on top form, abuzz with the excitement of the occasion, augmented by the thought of the summer holidays just minutes away. As we enter the marquee to do the deed, a parent comes up claiming that I was his French teacher at Westminster. It's good to see him.

'Oh,' I say half in jest. 'Did I actually teach you any?'

To my dismay, he says, 'No...but you did teach me about sonnets and I'll always be grateful for that.'

On the strength of this, I decide rashly between then and clambering onto the podium to scrap what I was going to say in my speech, and instead to compare the serried ranks of young people in front of me to a bunch of sonnets in the making. The substance of the poem is all there, the emotions ready for expression are there too, as are the words to enable this to take place even, but they still need to be properly arranged, the structure still needs polish, and that's the job of the school over the next several years. It all seems to make sense to me at the time, but whether it does to anyone else I just don't know.

The next day is my last day at Millfield. Parents' Day. We expect around 3,000 people on campus, and they start to materialize around 9. I hover around, rather like the Ancient Mariner, stopping one in three, parents and pupils, to chat about anything that's on their mind. It's the last bit of professional lurking I'll ever do, lurking being something that Heads do quite a lot as they indulge in what I have come to think of as MBL—management by lurking. Eventually everyone drifts towards the marquee and our last Parents' Day service gets under way. Julia then presents the prizes to the senior year, they present her with a gigantic bouquet of flowers, and then it's my turn. I try to thank everyone for the privilege of having been at the helm of their school for eight years, and for their support, while trying to include reference to as many of their astounding academic, musical, dramatic, sporting and other achievements as I can, while remaining aware that my audience's patience is not infinite, that the best speeches are the shorter ones and that lunch beckons.

To my surprise and gratification, this is followed by a standing ovation, which is followed by the arrival on stage of Nat Comer from the Lower Sixth, who bursts into a melodious and entirely unscheduled rendering of 'You'll never walk alone.' I join him in this and the whole event ends with our duet. Only later do I gather that vigilant members of staff have managed to prevent a stripogram from joining us in a trio. Rather a pity really, but I suppose that on these occasions three's a crowd. Then lunch with VIPs and governors, more speeches and farewells, and then onto the lawns to say goodbye to the seniors and their parents. The leavers all look stunning: the boys in Away Match dress and the girls in a variety of exotic and often remarkably small dresses. As at this time every year, these are inevitably the people I have got to know best, and as usual their departure leaves an imprecise fluttering in my chest. The chances of seeing them again are slim and I will miss them. So much potential, so much energy, so much goodwill. I suppose as one gets older as a teacher, one increasingly feeds off all this vibrant young life in an almost cannibalistic way.

Anyway, by early evening as the shadows start to lengthen, the campus starts to go quiet again and my love *affaire* with Millfield is just about over. Only 1,250 reports to do, and then I'm done too.